NOT WHAT I HAD IN MIND

A Motherhood Origin Story

Laura Diaz Freeland

Copyright © 2023 Laura Diaz Freeland
All rights reserved.
Hardcover ISBN: 979-8-9882373-0-3
eBook ISBN: 979-8-9882373-2-7

For my daughters, Vivienne and Margot, without whom I would be neither a mother nor a writer.

INTRODUCTION

My daughters had been in intensive care for 36 days when I walked past a woman smoking a cigarette at the bus stop in front of the hospital. She was young and thin everywhere except her (by my estimate) eight-months-pregnant belly—two months more pregnant than I had been when I delivered my daughters. I remember thinking, *this is bullshit. I swallowed that prenatal vitamin and choked down my vegetables, despite the dozen or more times a day I vomited. I made an OB appointment the moment the second line appeared on that pregnancy test. I wanted my babies, and I did everything I was supposed to do. And all I got was an emergency C-section and two very tiny, very sick little girls who are unlikely to survive.*

Smoking may have been that mother's vice, but rage was mine. I hated her for taking those extra months of pregnancy for granted. I can't think of anything I would not have done to protect my daughters for just a few extra weeks. I resented God for the injustice of his supposedly perfect plan. Why did I have to watch my daughters suffer—and probably die—while she would likely roll out of the hospital 24 hours after giving birth with a nine-pound, three-ounce baby in one arm and a cigarette in the opposite hand?

I wrote this whole narrative about her: she got pregnant when she wasn't even trying; she missed doctor's appointments; she had potato chips and vodka for dinner; she birthed a healthy baby and lived happily ever after. My version of her story villainized her. I was so wounded I could not imagine her wounds. I was entrenched in a suffering so painful I thought no one could understand, and I didn't want to see the challenges she faced because they looked self-inflicted from where I was standing.

I thought about her in the middle of the night when I would wake up in the blue hospital chair. I thought about her during my daughters' surgeries and again in the months I spent fighting to get our medical bills paid. *Why me?* I wondered. *Why not her?* In my mind, she came into motherhood unscathed, and I was bitter about it. The vision of her standing at that bus stop in her oh-so-pregnant glory haunted me.

I've had a lot of therapy since that day at the bus stop. These days, I wish I could have learned her story. I wonder where her baby's father was and why her mother didn't accompany her to the hospital that day. I think about how complicated life must be for a mother who has bigger things to worry about than giving up cigarettes. I recognize the commitment it takes to get to the hospital using our county's sad excuse for public transport. I couldn't see back then how the smoking mother and I are both imperfect in our own ways. I couldn't see that we are in this motherhood thing together, along with everyone who has ever carried a baby, be it inside or out.

Suffering has always been the plight of motherhood. Since the beginning of time, we have made impossible choices to protect our children. We have sacrificed our bodies, our time, our sanity, and even our lives. We have lost babies, lost our minds, and lost ourselves. Our stressors, cultures, families, and experiences may differ, but we are connected by the thread of wild love and lunacy it takes to raise children in this damaged and damaging world.

The words you're holding will not make sense of our suffering; they will not quell any anxiety, and may introduce some new ideas to fret over. But these words tell a story beyond my experiences. It's a story about how whatever version of motherhood we are dealt will, at some point, not be what we had in mind. And when that time comes, we may feel alone. But when the fog clears, we will find we are all in this terrifying, heartbreaking, beautiful mess together.

PART ONE: THE SLOW COOKER DIARIES

CHAPTER ONE

The Potential to Work

Medical terminology is almost always rooted in Greek or Latin. We find Greek words in clinical terminology like the *cardio* in cardiology or both the *gastro* and the *ectomy* in gastrectomy. Latin is used in prefixes and suffixes to indicate an anatomical location, like the *add* in adduction, which means away from, or *aemia* the root of anemia, which denotes a condition of the blood. For the healthy person with healthy children, it may seem unnecessary to understand the roots of medical terminology. But when we go from being a healthy person with healthy children to straddling the line between life and death, it helps to know the lingo.

December 14, 2019

    I am on the antepartum floor at Orlando Health Winnie Palmer Hospital for Women and Babies. *Ante* is Latin for before; *partum* is Latin for giving birth. This is the floor of the hospital reserved for women before they give birth. More specifically, it's reserved for women who need more time before they give birth. I am 22 weeks and four days pregnant. I need to buy myself 17 more weeks and three more days of pregnancy.

The magnesium sulfate drip in my arm and the betamethasone injection going into my thigh are not promising. My water hasn't broken, but I'm pretty sure I'm in labor. Though, no one has confirmed this. Maybe everyone is just hopeful the girls will calm down and I can go back to vomiting into my lap on my way to work every day.

A high-risk obstetrician comes into my room and tells me and my husband Jerod that when our daughters are born we have a choice to make: we can hold them while they pass peacefully or we can have them whisked away to the NICU in an attempt to keep them alive. Between my unmedicated contractions, he tells me if we choose intervention, it will be invasive. There will be breathing tubes and feeding tubes, IVs, and surgeries. Even then, there is no guarantee my daughters will have any quality of life. He says if they live, they may never walk, talk, or feed themselves; then he hands Jerod a pamphlet and asks if we have questions. I give him an 8/10 for his honesty and a 0/10 for his delivery.

It's hard to think with the searing pain of birth across my abdomen and lower back, but I'm trying. I'm trying to understand what would make anyone think that I—a woman with no medical background having the absolute worst day of my life—am equipped to make a decision such as this armed with nothing but a pamphlet.

I am sweating through the rise and fall of each contraction while considering the fact that there is no way to know whether my kids will live unless I give them a chance. Jerod writes the time and duration of each contraction. I consider a peaceful death. *Is it selfish to keep them alive? Is it faithless to let them die?* I need to decide quickly, seeing as how the children in question could make their debut at any moment, but I have no basis for it. All I have is this one doctor, unreliable internet search results, and—of course—the pamphlet. I wonder if someone could share this hospital's survival rates for babies born this early. *Do statistics even matter at this point? If we choose intervention, are we playing God or if we decline intervention, are we playing God? Does God even care if we play God?* I don't need a Master of Divinity to know there is no biblical instruction on whether to put your half-baked baby on life support.

Making a mother decide whether she wants her babies to suffer and probably die or not suffer and definitely die is an unusual form of cruelty. The torture is unintentional. It's also unbearable. They should have brought me a moral compass, not a fucking pamphlet.

Jerod calls his sister and her husband, an accomplished cardiologist, to tell them we are leaning toward not resuscitating. We want someone we trust to validate this decision. They are supportive while remaining cautiously neutral. It's like when you break up with a boyfriend and your friends suspect you might get back together. Your wisest friends know to empathize but never give their opinion, lest you end up marrying him later. After they hang up, my sister-in-law sends Jerod a link to a website with suggestions for what to do with your baby while she dies. It's both sweet and tragic.

We decide it would be selfish to put the twins through risky and invasive medical treatment. It is better for all of us if we let them go peacefully. We can mourn sooner. They won't suffer; hopefully we will suffer less than we would if we kept them alive long enough for us to grow attached only to watch them die later. Maybe we can even move past it in this lifetime, or maybe not. I already know I will never be pregnant again for fear I will find myself in this same place making this same decision.

When adults don't want to be resuscitated, we have to sign a Do Not Resuscitate (DNR) order. As parents who do not want our children resuscitated, we have to sign a DNR on our babies' behalf. Amid this chaos, a DNR is a sure thing. We can ensure our daughters will not die stressful, painful deaths. Without the DNR, we are in limbo. We don't know if they will live or die. If they live, we don't know if they will want to live. We can't predict if they will even have the cognitive capacity to know what they want. We don't know if our insurance is going to cover all of this or if we will lose our babies and our home. With a DNR, we know we will be newlyweds in our mid-30s who lost twin babies more than halfway through a pregnancy. It's woeful, but it's certain. Certainty is almost always less terrifying than the unknown.

I ask my nurse for the DNR and an epidural, but in the shuffle of moving to the labor and delivery floor to get said epidural, no one brings me the papers to sign. Jerod requests them again in the middle of the night. The DNR never comes, but we are too distraught to notice.

My mom and Jerod fall in and out of sleep in the hospital chairs, and I lie awake watching my contractions rise and fall on the monitors. It's been 16 hours and 57 minutes since I was admitted to the hospital. I tell my labor and delivery nurse I am going to vomit and a baby is going to come out. I am only three centimeters dilated and my water has not broken. She does not believe me. Typically, a mother's water breaks before she is in active labor, and three centimeters is not even a third of the way to fully dilated. I have convinced myself this is just pressure. I don't need to push. I will not push. The pressure feels serious though, so I yell at the nurse to get a real doctor. We urgently need an Actual MD in this room. This does not make her move any faster.

Like a scene from *Grey's Anatomy*, I open the puke bag and my mom lifts the hospital blanket off my legs. My first heave brings a splash of amniotic fluid that soaks her and splashes the wall. With my second heave, Vivienne Nora flies out of my body and lands between my knees on the hospital bed, weighing 570 grams—just one-pound and four ounces—and measuring barely a foot long. I don't get to see her, but I'll see her picture later. Her eyes are fused shut, her skin is translucent, and her head is full of hair. I will find the hair very weird and a little annoying. *Shouldn't your little body have been busy growing lungs instead of curly black hair?* With my third heave Vivienne's sister's water washes the walls, and my labor stops.

You would think when a one-pound baby delivers herself onto an unsterile hospital bed without a doctor in sight, the room would dissolve into chaos, but after Vivienne's birth, my world is small and quiet. The single second of shocked silence that comes over the room seems to go on for centuries before my mother whispers something about Vivienne trying to breathe. Jerod tells me she is beautiful. I do not believe him. A neonatal nurse scoops her up and manually pumps oxygen into her lungs until The Actual MD, a neonatologist, arrives with a respiratory therapist. There is no chaos. They take their places and move around my daughter like a dance.

The Actual MD comes as close as anyone has come to me in the four minutes since my daughter landed between my legs. He has glasses and silver hair and a warm, confident voice. He asks me what I want to do with my baby. His question—these words without a warning label—will change my life.

The level-headed thinker in me who chose a peaceful farewell 12 hours ago is gone. In her place is a mother who cannot live with herself if she doesn't at least try. I never got the DNR I requested, and I wonder if I had gotten it—if I had signed it—would The Actual MD be here to ask me what I want to do with Vivienne? I tell him he has to save her. He tells me he will try and then he is gone. I am left hoping my daughter will fight to live.

My daughter. I have a daughter. I threw up and a baby came out. I keep repeating this to anyone who will listen because it is incomprehensible. Repeating it does not make it any more believable, but I persist like a lunatic.

I chose the name Vivienne because I like the mouthfeel. Before I was ever pregnant, I knew if I had a daughter, she would be called Vivienne. I love the name so much. I haven't even looked up what it means, until now. In the aftermath of Vivienne's birth, I am immobile and trying to occupy my mind with anything but the trauma, so I search for the meaning of my daughter's name. The website TheBump tells me Vivienne is a girls' name derived from the Latin word *vivianus*. It means alive. I take this as a sign from God, and for a moment I am grateful for the DNR that never came.

NOT WHAT I HAD IN MIND

Peri is a word-forming element of Greek origin that means around or about. You see it a lot in medical terms like *pericardium*, which refers to the area around the heart and *perinatal*, which refers to the time around birth. Viable means that something (or, in this case, someone) has the potential to work. When we put those words together, we get *periviable*, which means my daughter was born around or about the time her body has potential to work. The problem with potential is it's usually unrealized.

The doctors and nurses who've spoken to me and my family don't use the word *periviable*. They seem to want parents to understand what's going on with their kids, while still preserving hope. Medical terminology does not lend itself to optimism. Instead of calling my daughter periviable, they call her a tiny baby. Which sounds cute, but there is nothing cute about her pellucid skin and long, skinny fingers.

I occasionally hear nurses use the word *micro preemie*. *Micro* comes from the Greek word *mikros*, meaning small. Small is an egregious understatement. Any baby born weighing under 800 grams before 26 weeks gestation is a micro preemie. If we're talking in terms of survival rates, Vivienne was born a lifetime before 26 weeks. *Micro* is an insufficient prefix.

When one twin is born, the logical progression is the birth of the second baby, so we wait. The hospital lobby becomes a waiting room for our friends, family, and even people we hardly know to pray and show support. They spread the word on social media, and before Vivienne is 24 hours old, news of her birth and critical status has spread to the literal other end of the planet.

I want to believe God cannot ignore the prayers of so many people. But I believe in the God who didn't stop Satan himself from having his way with Job, so I have my doubts.

We wait for Baby B for so long I am deemed stable and taken back to the antepartum floor where I have one job: to stay pregnant. I settle in. My husband goes downstairs to have lunch with a friend. The nurse tells me there is a terrace where I can get some fresh air once the doctor clears me—the same doctor who gave me the pamphlet. I can't wait.

When we go from a healthy person with healthy children to straddling the line between life and death, the new terminology we learn is mostly terrifying. The pace at which we learn is remarkable, and our ability to remain standing in the face of such desperation seems inhuman. When we're flirting with death while hoping for life, we find out what we're made of.

CHAPTER TWO

The People I Hate

When tragedy strikes, it feels like the world should stop for us. People should stop talking. Our bodies should stop expecting such luxuries as food, water, and sleep. Instead, people keep sending emails and text messages. They show up in hospital rooms trying to do their jobs. When everything is all wrong, it's brazen of the world to just keep spinning.

December 17, 2019

In an emergency, it takes 18 minutes to go from pregnant on the fifth floor to not pregnant on the second floor. I wish I didn't know this. I was just talking to a nice nurse about getting some fresh air on the antepartum terrace. I was planning to stay pregnant long enough to say I had identical twins born in different years, and the next thing I knew I was traveling full speed toward the elevators in my hospital bed screaming at God. The rest of the patients on the floor probably thought I was being rushed to the psych ward, not the OR. Eighteen minutes later, Margot Midiam was born via emergency

C-section exactly 17 weeks before her due date. I never got my fresh air on the antepartum terrace.

I am in purgatory now: a postoperative recovery room, complete with a lactation consultant teaching me how to use a hospital grade breast pump to draw milk out of my body and into two-ounce bottles. She is short with crunchy blonde hair and is old enough that she has not pumped breast milk in at least 35 years. I am not even sure I am alive, let alone capable of operating boob-pumping machinery, but apparently making breastmilk is more important than having a pulse. She gives me lanolin for my nipples and tells me to center them perfectly in the flange. She pushes one button and then another, and I feel a mechanical pull where my babies should be latched. After a few minutes, a single drop of milk falls into one of the bottles. It's thick and yellow. She tells me this is colostrum, and she is delighted. I am certain my daughters are going to starve. She assures me this is all they will need and instructs me to keep it cold and drop it off at the window on the left on my way into the NICU. There, they will prepare it to be dripped through a tube down my daughters' throats. I wonder if she is insane, as the drop of milk at the bottom of this bottle will definitely evaporate before it makes it out of the bottle and down a tube. If by some holy of holies miracle it doesn't evaporate, it's certainly not a shareable portion.

The breast pump has so many buttons and so many parts. My mom jots notes. I am grateful I will not need to remember how to attach duckbills to flanges later. I want the lactation consultant to go away—to leave me and my exposed boobs, my mutilated body, and my low blood pressure alone—but she just keeps talking about pumping every two hours and logging milliliters and labeling bottles. She goes on about liquid gold and how pumping often will help my milk come in. She stresses we need to sterilize everything in a bag in the microwave. I wonder how long I would have to microwave the bag to make it melt. I wonder if when my daughters die, my boobs will be full of milk, and I wonder how long it will take to dry up. *Will it hurt? How long will my engorged breasts remind me of the daughters I won't get to raise?*

In Greek mythology, Apollo removed Asclepius, the god of medicine, from his mother's abdomen. Cesarean sections are recorded in ancient literature from around the world. Before this surgery was ever used to save mothers and babies, the Romans performed C-sections because their religious beliefs barred them from burying pregnant women. The first C-section on a living woman was performed in 1610, but until the second half of the 19th century, the vast majority of women who had C-sections died. I am grateful to have had my daughter in a sterile operating room with blood on standby.

To cut a baby from the womb, an obstetrician makes an incision across the lower abdomen through seven layers of skin, fat, muscle, and protective tissue. The surgeon makes a second incision through the uterus to remove the baby. This incision, like the first, is usually horizontal and low on the uterus, but in preterm labor it's difficult to access the lower part of the uterus, and there is a risk the baby's head will get trapped during contractions. Instead of a low, horizontal incision, the uterus is cut vertically down the middle. This is called a classical incision and it's the only way to do a C-section for extremely premature infants.

The thing no one tells you about C-sections is that *incision* is a term used mostly for the patient's comfort. What actually happens is the surgeons rip the uterus in half with their hands. They make a tiny cut; they tell you you're going to feel a tugging sensation, and then two grown adults each grab half a uterus and pull. It's insane! They do this because a jagged incision stitched together is more structurally sound under pressure than a precise incision stitched together. The jagged incision reduces the risk of uterine rupture in future pregnancies.

The surgeon who tore my uterus in half with his bare (gloved) hands stops by to explain this whole ripping thing to me, and a laugh escapes from the depths of my butchered body. I assure him there will be no future pregnancies. He says, "Well, you never know." I press my lips into a mean girl smile and hope he reads minds—or at least body language.

When you have a C-section, they expect you to get up and walk as soon as you can feel your feet again. I cannot understand this, as trying to scoot my butt up one inch on the bed makes me feel like I will split open and my guts will fall out. It has been just a few hours since my second-born daughter was whisked away to the NICU in a plastic box—just a few hours since my insides were torn in half on the outside, and I have to stand up because the nurse says I will recover faster. We are living in alternate realities because I know I will never recover from this.

The social worker pops her head in. I cringe. She came after Vivienne was born to talk me through birth certificates and social security numbers. I wanted her to leave then and I want her to leave now. She either does not notice or does not give a shit that I am screaming on the inside for her to leave. She goes through the whole birth certificate and social security spiel again, and now she is talking about the baby blues. She says I ought to talk to my doctor if my blues last more than a week or two. *My kids are going to die. If I'm only sad for a week or two, wouldn't that make me deranged?* My mom implies that maybe it's time for the social worker to leave. The social worker thinks I should go to therapy. I think she should go to hell.

My father, my mother, and my brother have made themselves as comfortable as they can, considering this room is a revolving door of medical personnel. Jerod arrives from the NICU bearing a printed photograph of Margot. She is intubated and bloody. Her eyes are fused shut like her sister's. I feel a surge of nausea. "She looks dead," I tell him. This makes everyone uncomfortable. I break the awkward silence by sending Jerod back up to the NICU. Someone should be there with our two helpless daughters, and I cannot do it. I have nothing to give them, but I hope he does.

Jerod leaves. My mom holds the photo of Margot, and something about the way she looks at it compels me to open my mouth and confess, "I don't want to love them because they're just going to die." My voice is callous, but inside I am fighting to stuff down grief, sadness, anger, guilt, fear, and probably some other feelings I can't yet name. Everyone's eyes widen, but no one says anything. It's not exactly the kind of thing you can disagree with, so we sit there in awkward silence until the dietitian pops her head into the room and raps on the door.

I want to run to the bathroom and hide there forever, but if I ran anywhere, my guts would fall out. I glare at the curtain and dare the dietitian to come in. Her blonde curls are pulled back into a ponytail and she is very pregnant and very familiar. A lifetime ago, she trained me to fold and sell luxury Lycra at my nights-and-weekends job. I soften my glare and she sets down a gift bag on the table in front of my bed. She says she hopes it's OK that she came by. She asked a mutual friend if she thought I would be comfortable with her visit; our friend insisted The Pregnant Dietitian come see me.

The Pregnant Dietitian is everything the lactation consultant and the social worker are not. She gingerly steps into this uncomfortable, emotional space where I am traumatized but trying not to grieve. I can tell her heart hurts for me, but she is composed. She is encouraging, but not delusional, about the likely outcome of my predicament. She is empathetic but does not let her feelings take up the space where my feelings should be. She does not ignore the photos of my one-pound babies sitting on the shelf, nor does she pry. She hands me a big bag with useful gifts. I love her, but she has work to do, and the palliative care doctor is waiting in line to see me.

This is not the first time I've met this scrawny, straight-haired palliative care doctor with an accent I can't place. He was among the first to visit me after Vivienne was born. The first time he came, he asked if I was familiar with the term "palliative care." I cried as I confirmed that I knew palliative care is comfort care for the dying, and I assumed he was in my room mere minutes after my daughter's birth to tell me she was dying. He didn't say that, but he didn't not say it. He told me he and his team were there to ensure Vivienne's comfort. I am not sure why he has to give me the same speech again, but I'm sure I hate him.

The bag the Pregnant Dietitian delivered is full of designer disposable underwear, herb-infused maxi pads, a book of prayers, and a pumping bra. Her visit and this bag do not seem profound on the surface, but she has just shown me how to walk into someone's grief with grace. Few people do this well. I know because my hospital room has been a turnstile of failed attempts at empathy. Looming loss and death make people super weird. They ignore the photos of almost-dead babies on the shelf and talk about the weather or they tell me it will all be OK. It's hard to tell if they are trying to make me feel better or if they are trying to ease their own discomfort. I can tell who has experienced trauma or grief or had enough therapy to emotionally evolve. They are the ones who bring gifts and let me talk or not talk. They understand there is nothing they can say to make me feel better, so they don't even try, and I appreciate that about them.

When the Postpartum Interrogation Committee finally stops checking my vitals and assessing my risk for postpartum depression, my parents, my husband, and my brother come to sit with me. My room has a floor-to-ceiling window overlooking a concrete slab. It's not the antepartum terrace I had hoped for, but it will have to do. There's a pull-out couch made of blue, medical grade, sterilization-friendly fabric where my mom intends to sleep for the rest of her life, since we are all going to die here. I don't want to talk or think, and I definitely don't want to cry, so I put on the pumping bra the Pregnant

Dietitian brought me and I make the lactation consultant proud.

While it seems wrong for life to go on when our hearts are so broken that our bodies refuse to cooperate, maybe this is what we need. When people do their jobs or step into our grief to encourage us, it feels invasive and even dismissive, but it reminds us that the world is still spinning, and if we are to live, we have to spin with it. It doesn't have to be our finest work or our best life. We just have to get up.

CHAPTER THREE

The Declaration

We are fickle. We can wake up with the highest of expectations and something as quotidian as spilled coffee can wreck our hopes and dreams. Alternatively, we can find ourselves so pessimistic about our circumstances that we intentionally stave off hope. We think we can protect ourselves from pain by expecting it. Instead of anticipating a miracle, we envision burials.

December 20, 2019

I just rode the elevator down seven floors to the NICU wearing a hospital robe and pushing an empty wheelchair, just in case I need it for the return trip. I am not the first NICU mom to make this journey, but something about this scene makes me feel more like a psych patient than a new mother.

I park my wheelchair outside the door to my daughters' double room in Pod 1 of the NICU. I peer into one incubator and then into the other. I've been here just a few times since the girls were born. It nearly paralyzes me to see these impossibly tiny beings with their heart beats visible through their chests. I wonder how many people have seen a living baby at just 23 weeks gestation.

A tall, olive-skinned doctor with curly hair and rectangular glasses steps into the room. "Hi, Mom," he says. That's what everyone calls me here. Part of me wonders if they do this just so they don't have to remember anyone's name, but my name is printed on everything—the hospital bracelet, the babies' beds, the chart. They can glance in any direction for a reminder of my name, but they call me mom, as if to remind me I'm a mother now, even though it doesn't feel like it. In the presence of my daughters, words are beyond my reach. All I can muster is a nod to acknowledge the doctor is speaking to me.

"The babies are doing good today," he says with a Spanish accent. "They are critical, but they are stable." He explains to me how the first seven to ten days of a tiny baby's life are very telling. This period is when babies declare themselves—they tell you whether they plan to fight for life or whether they are too weak to try. He acknowledges my daughters are very small and very sick, but I still get the feeling he is rooting for my tiny twins. In a world where most people expect my daughters to die, he sounds hopeful. It's not optimism per se, but rather a passion for what's possible. I cannot summon passion for possibility right now. I am too scared to hope, so my expression is blank. I nod again, and The Possibility Doctor bids me goodbye.

My mother is a slight woman standing not even an inch over five feet tall. She listens more than she speaks. She is gentle and patient, but she is not weak. She does not sugar coat truth or deny reality. Her world has come crashing down many times in her 59 years of life, but she always rebuilds. She always finds a way to move forward—to believe in the possibility that something good will come from adversity.

Today is Discharge Day. When I arrive back to my hospital room, mom has the room organized, packed, and loaded onto a cart. I cannot fathom the next steps; nonetheless, with my mother's help, I am moving forward. Someone is coming with a wheelchair to take me downstairs. Someone is coming to take me away from my daughters.

A petite brunette arrives to load the cart and delivers me to the lobby. The sun is beaming through the windowed dome that makes this lobby so impressive. When Jerod pulls up in his Toyota 4Runner, I notify the Petite Brunette of his arrival. She wheels me out the doors and, for the first time in five days, I am outside the hospital walls. Christmas is just days away, but even in my short sleeve dress, the Florida heat is stifling. In the valet loop, another mother is waiting in a wheelchair to get into her ride. Next to her, her husband and the hospital's Committee for Real and Actual Car Seat Safety buckle her rosy-cheeked baby boy into a car seat. I think to myself, *that cannot be a newborn.* He is gargantuan. The husband and The Committee click Big Bubba's seat into its base. His mother pops out of her wheelchair like only someone who did not birth her 102-pound toddler via emergency C-section can. She simply gets into the car and buckles herself in next to her newborn teenager.

Jerod steps out of his car and comes around to open the passenger door. The Petite Brunette offers her arm as support, but I tell her I think it's easier if I use the armrests. I dig deep for the strength of the thousands of chaturangas I have done in my decade of practicing yoga and I press my palms into the armrests of my wheelchair to lift myself out of the seat. I waddle to the car and I stop to stare at the open car door. I do not understand how I am supposed to step up into my husband's monster truck. *What was he thinking when he bought this? This is not a family vehicle. It's an abomination.* I turn around and back my butt up to the side of the seat to evaluate how far up I need to get to rest my rear on the passenger seat. By my estimate, it's about 37 inches above sea level.

With my back to the car, I rest my palms on the passenger seat like I'm about to do a tricep dip. (I am most definitely not going to do a tricep dip.) I channel my chaturangas, but the cushioned seat is too soft. I have no leverage. Jerod suggests he just pick me up. I suggest he just head inside and have a C-section real quick. We settle on a maneuver in which I brace myself with my palms on the edge of the seat and he lifts my legs into the car while I support my upper body and try not to lose my guts. We are successful. He closes the door. I apply pressure to my lower belly to keep my insides inside, and I sob. This is not the motherhood I imagined.

I was only six weeks pregnant when I had my first ultrasound. A few months prior, we lost a baby to a complicated miscarriage that ended in an emergent D & C. When I fell pregnant again, my obstetrician opted for an early ultrasound to keep me safe. I was afraid we would get bad news again, so I did what any well-adjusted woman in her 30s would do: I asked my mom to come with me instead of my husband.

With my mom politely looking away—as if she didn't bring me into the world stark naked—I stripped and put on the paper gown. The ultrasound technician prepped the wand for a transvaginal ultrasound. I put my feet in the stirrups. She wove the wand around and found a baby with a heartbeat. She took a few measurements and she wove the wand around again. We were all quiet for a moment, our eyes bouncing back and forth between one another. At six weeks, an embryo looks like a dense white spot in a sea of salt and pepper, and this ultrasound appeared to have two distinctly embryo-looking spots. "Oh, there's another baby," the tech said, sounding nothing like a person delivering life-altering news.

After the ultrasound, my obstetrician sat me down to set realistic expectations for this pregnancy. He was as surprised as I was about the two embryos growing in my uterus. It looked like the babies were sharing an amniotic sac, making it the riskiest of twin pregnancies, but there was still a chance a membrane would develop between them. Multiple babies automatically makes a pregnancy high-risk; it also increases the chance of premature birth. As if that were not enough, he warned my mother and me about vanishing twin syndrome—so early in a twin pregnancy, there is a possibility that one baby will just disappear. It's a partial miscarriage where the first embryo's tissue gets absorbed by the mother or the surviving twin. This syndrome was the cause of my insomnia for the three weeks that followed.

I asked Jerod to come home from work early the day of the ultrasound. I covered one of the babies with my thumb while pointing to one baby on the ultrasound photo. "There's our baby," I said. He smiled, and I waited a long and awkward 27 seconds before I removed my thumb and announced, "and there is our other baby."

He told me to shut up and we laughed. We laughed for weeks. In between laughter, I prayed for two little girls. I dreamed of bows bigger than their heads and miniature versions of grown-up clothing. In my head, I dressed them in neutrals and added pops of color with shoes and bonnets. I was eleven weeks pregnant when I found out they were girls. I bought all the delicate neutrals, oversized bows, and nightgowns with woodland creatures I could find.

Fifty to sixty percent of multiples are born before 37 weeks gestation. I expected prematurity. I expected the NICU. I just didn't expect *this*. I didn't expect tissue paper babies on the brink of death. I didn't anticipate what it would feel like to watch another mother climb into the backseat with her baby when I may never see mine alive again. Here, in the pseudo-safety of this monster truck I hate, I expel five days of pent-up hysteria in the form of salt water and snot. Jerod knows he cannot fix this, so he doesn't try. I love this about him.

My catharsis ends in time for Jerod to pull into our driveway. He opens his door and steps out of the car like any normal person would do. I panic a little at the thought of disembarking. I consider staying in the car—just for a day or two—until I've healed enough that the step down doesn't resemble Everest, but I know no one is going to go for this idea. Jerod offers his hands; instead, I opt for the oh-shit handle above the door. I pick up my legs with my hands and turn them sideways. I support my weight on this tiny plastic handle and slide my broken body down the side of the passenger's seat, depositing myself safely on the Earth. I suggest we sell The Monster Truck.

NOT WHAT I HAD IN MIND

For two days, I do nothing but sleep, eat, and pump. On my second night home, Jerod calls me from the hospital to tell me both the girls' bellies are dusky. I'm not sure what this means, but I am sure it's cause for panic. The doctors suspect bowel perforations. They ask for consent to place drains into their intestines to see if this resolves the problem. I am sitting on the couch with my mother and brother when Jerod calls. None of us breathe. I ask how the drains work and whether the girls will be under anesthesia when they place the drains. I ask how we will know if the drains solve the problem; how long will we wait before we take next steps? What are the next steps? Jerod doesn't have answers to my questions. He is overwhelmed. He didn't think to ask.

I press my palms into the edge of the couch cushion and slide myself onto the floor. I lie prone on the living room rug and I scream into the floor because that must be where God lives these days. "Do not take my daughters, please take me instead," I sob aloud, and the place where my belly is stitched together aches.

For the rest of the night, I pump, but I do not eat or sleep. When moonlight turns to sunlight, Jerod calls to say the drains did not work. My daughters will have surgery today.

In 2015, my friend and roommate, Kelli, told me we could not remain roommates unless I could appreciate her *Grey's Anatomy* references. We binge watched every season, and when there were no new episodes left, I missed my friends, McDreamy, McSteamy, and the dark and twisty Meredith Grey, so I started the series all over again.

The second time I watched *Grey's Anatomy*, Jerod and I had just started dating. How could he truly know me if he didn't know these beloved characters? The second time around, I noticed details I had missed the first time, and I grew attached to different characters. For the uninitiated, in the fifth season, a new pediatric surgeon rolls in on tennis shoes that double as roller skates. She is blonde, energetic, and brilliant. She is Arizona Robbins. When Jerod calls to tell me about the surgery, I ask him which doctor he talked to. He tells me she's a neonatologist I haven't met yet. She was on vacation when the twins were born, but she knows everything about them. He says she is The Real Life Arizona Robbins.

This Arizona Robbins does not arrive on roller-skates, but she is the perfect character to get attached to right now. When she broke the news to Jerod about the bowel perforations and the surgery, he asked if the girls could die. She straight up said yes. No sugar, no milk, just yes. I give her 20/10 for honesty and delivery.

I manage to peel myself out of my chair. I take the saddest steps to my bedroom, where I think about changing into a fresh nightgown, but decide it's too much work. I do the sad-mom shuffle back to the living room where my parents are waiting to take me to the hospital. Life is happening in slow motion because I can only move in slow motion. My body and my brain are protesting the physical and emotional stress of the last week, and while I am frustrated at how long it takes me to get from the car to the hospital doors, I cannot will myself to move any faster.

When we arrive in the NICU, Vivienne and Margot are already being prepped for surgery—a surgery that will be performed in their double room in the NICU.

NOT WHAT I HAD IN MIND

The high-frequency jet ventilator that breathes for them doesn't lend itself to travel, so they can't make the voyage to an actual operating room. Jerod is in the waiting room with his parents. We take our seats with them. Shortly after, a surgeon with hands bigger than the twins' bodies comes to tell me he is going to cut them open and pull out their intestines to assess the damage. He tells us he may open them up and find there is nothing he can do. What he means is he may open them and find they are going to die today.

Vivienne goes first. She has two bowel perforations. Behemoth Hands gives her an ileostomy, a hole in her abdomen where a piece of the last section of the small intestine sticks out. She will poop from her ileostomy until she is bigger. Barring any other complications, he plans to reconnect her ileum to her colon in a few months. He seems pleased to have found mostly healthy bowel, but he cannot stay to chat because he has to start Margot's surgery. When he opens Margot, he finds three bowel perforations. He gives her a jejeunostomy—a hole in her abdomen where a piece of her jejeunom, the part of the small intestine between the duodenum and the ileum, sticks out. She will poop from her jejeunostomy until she is bigger. If all goes well, he will do a partial re-connection in a few months. He hopes to put her all the way back together sometime after she turns one. In purgatory, nothing is ideal, but nothing is less ideal than death, so I will take these living babies, albeit with some assembly required.

The doctors, nurses, and respiratory therapists do everything in their power to maintain patients' privacy, but we share rooms and we share walls. We see who comes and who goes. We may not know each other's names, but we hear each other's pain. I know three babies had exploratory abdominal surgery today, and I know only two babies are still alive. My daughters have declared themselves.

CHAPTER FOUR

More Miracles for a Hundred Thousand, Please and Amen

The brain is arguably our most important organ. It tells the rest of the body what to do. It controls how we think and feel and communicate. It is an intricate wonder that can rewire itself and even heal itself from trauma. It figures out how to get the job done, unless it can't. In a society that defines success according to accomplishments, a brain that can't do its job is a terrifying prospect.

December 24, 2019

    Vivienne is wearing the world's tiniest Santa hat. Her hand is closed around the tip of my thumb; four of her five fingers rest on my nail. It is incomprehensible something so small could be fully functional. Truth be told, it's too soon to tell if any part of my daughters is fully functional, but when I look at them I see whole babies. They are miniature, but from the outside it appears they have everything they need to live. A lot of possibilities exist between alive and dead, though.

Since the day I ditched the DNR and told the The Actual MD to save Vivienne, I've swatted away the thoughts of complications, disabilities, and daunting unknowns. I am already sinking in the murky water of trauma and postpartum depression. I cannot carry another burden, but today is judgment day. I may not have a choice.

The prefix *neuro* is of Greek origin. It means nerve or nerves. Nerves are groups of cells that send electrical signals to tell our bodies to move or to feel. We have nerve cells all over our bodies, but the highest concentration of neurons is on our brains. *Sono* comes from the Latin *sonus*, meaning sound, and *gram* comes from the Greek word *gramma*, which means written or drawn.

Today, a technician will perform a *neurosonogram* on each of my daughters. Using sound waves to capture an image of the brain, our doctors will be able to see whether their brains are bleeding. I don't need a medical degree to know that if I don't want my kids' fingers or noses to bleed, I *definitely* don't want their brains to bleed.

Extremely premature babies have underdeveloped brains with fragile blood vessels that are liable to rupture, causing an intraventricular hemorrhage (IVH), also known as a brain bleed. The brain is remarkably adaptable. Sometimes babies with bleeds grow up and live typical lives, and sometimes they don't.

Vivienne flails her matchstick legs. I pump foaming hand sanitizer into my hands and rub vigorously. I repeat these steps twice more before opening the isolette and cupping her head so delicately that I don't actually touch her. She settles, but my mind does not. *Who will she be? Who will I have to become to raise her?*

NOT WHAT I HAD IN MIND

The purpose of the neurosonogram is to look for abnormalities so that we, the parents, can get an idea of the quality of life our daughters are expected to have. The doctors need to ensure there is nothing they need to treat; they are also ensuring we have all the information we need to decide how hard we want to fight for our children. We have to consider how complicated and taxing we want our lives—and theirs—to be. This is about so much more than chauffeuring twins to doctors' appointments and therapies for the rest of their lives. This raises a question I don't have the answer to: How do you raise a child who knows she is valuable in a culture that idolizes and rewards the sharpest and most able-bodied among us?

Society has come a long way in how we accommodate and include people with disabilities, but the prospect of learning to be a mother was sufficiently intimidating *before* there were two babies born too soon. Now I may need to mother atypical children in a world that is trying, but still failing, to make accommodations for them and for me.

I want a miracle. I want kids with fully functional brains that aren't bleeding, and even though this is what every mom wants, I feel like an asshole for wanting it. My daughters are so likely to have intellectual disabilities and developmental delays that it feels wrong to pray for something different. It feels like I'm praying for them to be something other than what they are.

I wash my hands with soap and water, followed by hand sanitizer, and I slide my hands into Margot's bed. She doesn't have a Santa hat, which seems unfair. I ask the nurse if they have another one, and when she goes to check, I sing the first few words of Lauren Daigle's "Light of The World." "The world waits for a miracle," comes out as a whisper, and the tears come. I don't want to let myself feel this. I know the heartache will render me even more useless than I already am. I close Margot's doors and abruptly end my visit.

I spend most of my time at home vacillating between numbness and desperation in my remote-controlled chair. I can push the down arrow to recline all the way back for my frequent naps, or I can use the up arrow to lift the seat of the chair and tilt it forward until it drops me safely onto the ground. My dad and Jerod found the chair on Craigslist. It's supposed to be for seniors with knee problems, but it should really be marketed as a C-section chair. From the chair, I scroll endlessly through social media. I buy pajamas, leggings, and spare pump parts from the advertisements served to me. I get my dopamine where I can.

Occasionally, reality hits and tears stream down my face. I whisper prayers under my breath. *Please, God, let me raise my daughters. Let their little brains be OK. Give us a miracle.* Most of the time it feels like I'm whispering prayers into the abyss, but I didn't expect my daughters to live for an hour and they've been alive an entire week. I want this to mean God hears us and he's delivering on our pleas for miracles, but I am keeping my distance from my daughters. Their fragility scares me. It forces me to face everything I thought I believed about God.

My maternal grandfather was a fire and brimstone preacher. I may as well have been born on the pew of a Baptist church in Union City, New Jersey. I know what the Bible says about grace, but I heard what people whispered behind the backs of pregnant teenagers and divorcées in church. I learned that Jesus loves me no matter what, but the people teaching me about Jesus made it seem like certain sins (namely drugs, sex, and the word *fuck*) were unforgivable. But I was curious about said sins. Rather than be a lukewarm Christian, which was *definitely* the worst thing I could be, I decided that when I grew up, I wouldn't be a Christian at all. What God deems unforgivable doesn't matter if you don't believe he's real.

A lot of life has happened between 18 and now. I fell down and apart. I pushed God away until I didn't. I pulled myself back to faith while wondering if maybe I shouldn't. I cultivated an understanding of grace and of a God who knows we cannot get it together and forgives us in advance. I also inadvertently developed the idea that a good God will give me good things if I follow him closely. It's human nature to want something from God. Most of us expect our commitment to him to be beneficial in some way. *I'll give you my devotion and my best behavior if you'll give me the life I want.*

Now I'm here, in my remote-controlled C-section chair praying and pondering what it means to both believe God can do impossible things and know he might not. He might not spare my daughters' brains, and if he doesn't, I'm supposed to, in theory, believe he is still good. But even if he spares my daughters, he won't spare all the babies born too soon. And I cannot make this make sense.

I pick up my phone and open my text messages, just in case I missed something from Jerod or my dad. No news. I wiggle my way onto my side and close my eyes, but I'm too uncomfortable and too uneasy to sleep. The phone vibrates; with it comes a surge of adrenaline I feel from my gray roots to my peeling toenail polish. Once I know what's in this text message, I can't unknow it. It could change the way I see my daughters, and it could change what I believe about God.

Jerod's message says, "only grade one bleeds." This is good news. It's the most mild type of bleed. He offers to conference me into his conversation with The Possibility Doctor, but I'm scared I'll hear something I don't want to know. I ask him to just text me a summary. I watch the three dots indicating he is typing. A full minute later, another message comes through explaining my daughters' bleeds are so insignificant that sometimes full-term babies are born with bleeds like this and they go undetected. My father will later tell me that The Possibility Doctor told him when he sees a neurosonogram like this on one tiny baby, he celebrates. The fact we got two is a watershed worthy of Veuve.

Like a Hallmark Channel Original, I got my Christmas miracle on Christmas Eve. This merits a shower and the billowy black maxi dress peppered with gold cheetah spots, originally purchased for the baby shower I never had. I pack my breast pump because, now that I'm doing this, I have to do it all the time or I will explode. With the finesse of a toddler who's just learned to climb, I clamber into The Monster Truck to head to a Christmas Eve church service. *Why do we still own this vehicle?*

We pull out of our driveway and pass our neighbors' homes lit with holiday cheer. For a fraction of a second it feels like Christmas; then I remember our own

NOT WHAT I HAD IN MIND

Christmas lights, half strung because Jerod was going to finish lighting the shrubs the afternoon I went into labor. I remember the last time I rode in this car on these streets still pregnant with two little girls. My memories will forever be governed by this line of demarcation: before and after the extremely premature and traumatic birth of my daughters. This one experience will shape who I am for the rest of my life.

It's isolating to be living this nightmare dotted with miracles while the rest of the world drinks hot chocolate and exchanges gifts. My feelings of isolation and desperation are very real, but if I step out from behind my lens, I can see a shared experience. Traumatic or not, motherhood changes everyone. We can only speculate about what kind of mothers we think we are going to be—how we will or will not change—but when the baby comes, all bets are off. We don't know how the drama or the trauma or the hormones will drive our approach to mothering. Maybe we will hand our babies off to strangers or maybe we won't let anyone hold them until they are three years old. Maybe motherhood will mellow us or maybe it will propel us into a state of perpetual anxiety. One way or the other, it has a profound effect on all of us.

We arrive at church and, as though we have an unspoken escape plan in the event of an emotional breakdown, Jerod, my parents, and his parents slip into the very back row nearest an exit. The lights dim and the first measure of a song plays. I know what's coming. I hold my breath. The velvety and familiar voice of a friend sings, "The world waits for a miracle; the heart longs for a little bit of hope." My exhalation is a sob that turns into a hysterical cry. "The drought breaks with the tears of a mother. A Baby's cry is the sound of love," Velvet Voice continues. Now would be the time to use that unspoken escape plan, but no one moves. An hour later, I sneak out before my family to milk myself in a room reserved for pumping and nursing mothers. Technically, I meet the criteria, but *mother* doesn't feel like the right word.

The word *mother* seems simple on the surface. It's a woman who cares for a child or children who belong to her. Even if I had an iota of mental health left (which, I don't) I wouldn't be able to care for my daughters. I cannot feed them from my breasts or from a bottle. I cannot lay them on my chest for comfort. I cannot clothe them, and I'm terrified I will break them if I change their diapers. This is not motherhood.

I thought coming to church on Christmas Eve would give me a semblance of normal, but being here makes me anxious. Being here makes me realize there is no normal for me anymore. I don't want to see anyone I know. I don't want to talk about our situation. I don't want them to look at me with sad faces. It turns out, I didn't come to church for normalcy. I came to church because it seems like the kind of thing you should do when you need God on your side—when you need a hundred thousand more miracles.

I usher my family out of the building with the urgency of a mama duck traversing a busy road with her ducklings, and I ask Jerod to take me to the hospital. Clinically, nothing has changed since I last saw my girls, but the neurosonogram gave me permission to hope.

In the girls' room, I wash my hands and then sanitize them again before entering Vivienne's world. I close my eyes and raise a hallelujah for two beautiful brains, but I feel just a hint of shame. *How can my relief be right when there is so much going wrong just outside these doors? What would I have done if, instead of news worthy of a toast, the results had been ruinous?*

I have been begging for miracles, believing the best, preparing for the worst, marinating in spiritual turmoil, and feeling an abundance of guilt over every potential outcome. I got my miracles today, but the guilt and spiritual turmoil seem to be here to stay.

When we become mothers, we don't know anything about the way our baby's brain will work. Even if we have a neurosonogram to tell us everything is perfectly normal, we have no clue who they will be. Yet they are the most precious thing in the world to us. They have value simply because they exist and they are ours. A trillion things can go wrong in the building of a brain, and even if they do, a mother's love is always right.

CHAPTER FIVE

Dust, Sweat, Blood, and Flesh-Eating Fungus

Professor, author, and world famous shame researcher Brené Brown opens her book "*Daring Greatly*" with a passage from Theodore Roosevelt's speech, "*Citizenship in a Republic.*" In this speech, Roosevelt gives credit to "the man who is actually in the arena, whose face is marred by dust and sweat and blood." Brown goes on to write about how this idea of being in the arena is the embodiment of vulnerability. When you're in the arena, it is messy and scary and you don't know if you will win or you will lose. It's not winning or losing that matters, though; it's showing up for the fight.

January 2020

I'm standing in the doorway of a super sterile, rectangular hospital room. In the middle of the room is a plastic slow cooker. Instead of food, it will cook a half-baked baby into a well-done one—if I'm lucky. To the left of the door, there is an oversized blue recliner made of medical grade fabric, the kind that is easily disinfected and would stick to your bare thighs if you were wearing shorts. There's a noisy, high frequency ventilator with 298 buttons in the far left corner and a tower of medication pumps on each side of the slow cooker. I suspect the wound care nurse who just arrived is slightly claustrophobic, because, despite her slight frame, she turns sideways to get past the slow cooker. She and I are dressed in personal protective equipment (PPE). My mouth and nose are covered with a mask, my hands are gloved and my long and dirty hair is tucked into a cap. The one-size-fits-most disposable robe is so long I use the two extra feet of fabric to tie a bow around my calves. The nurse sets her supplies on sterile gauze on top of the slow cooker. She washes her hands, gloves up, and opens the portals into Vivienne's sterile little world.

Vivienne is 19 days old, 24 weeks and 5 days gestation when corrected for prematurity. This means I should still be pregnant with her for at least another 10 weeks, preferably 15. That was the goal, anyway. Yet, here we are. A week ago, one of Vivienne's NICU nurses mentioned a couple of tiny white spots on her back. She got my consent to biopsy them, and she told me it was probably nothing. I believed her. Rookie mistake. I never saw the spots because they kept Vivienne on her back for her first 10 days of life, a protocol the hospital uses to reduce the risk of brain bleeds. By the time the biopsy came back positive for aspergillus, the tiny white dots had turned into four, inch-long oblong wounds on Vivienne's back and down to her tiny baby butt, where the flesh-eating fungus had started to feast on the muscle. Note to self: do not believe a nurse who says it's probably nothing. Zero points for honesty.

NOT WHAT I HAD IN MIND

When the nurse removes Vivienne's bandage, the carnage leaves me breathless and nauseous. I need a moment outside, but if I leave, even for a second, I have to put new protective gear on all over again. Instead, I put my hands into the portals opposite the slight, blonde, wound-care nurse. I delicately cup Vivienne's head, which seems smaller than a tennis ball. I'm inclined to rub her hair with my thumb, but more than a dozen people have told me to avoid that impulse. Her skin and her nervous system are too fragile for this kind of affection. She is wet tissue paper, and I am terrified I will be the one to tear her.

I keep my hand still and I swallow tears as I watch the nurse irrigate and debride the wounds with saline, and cotton swabs, and tweezers. The wounds, our hands, and even the cotton swabs look massive next to her periviable body. When the nurse is done, she packs the lesions with gauze, and I notice Vivienne is crying. We can't hear her because of the endotracheal tube down her throat, but her mouth is open and her face is contorted. My daughter doesn't have a voice yet, but she already has something to say about her suffering.

From Hollywood to classic literature, the sound of a baby's first cry is a momentous occasion, teeming with emotion. There is the relief that the baby is on the outside and breathing. There is pride and joy and disbelief that you grew a complete, living human. A single sound ushers elation into the world. When that sound does not come, terror fills the void. I've tried to distance myself, but it's too late. I am traumatized. I am terrified of what will happen. I am scared to hurt her and I am scared to love her.

The nurse closes the slow cooker and tells me my daughter did great. Vivienne promptly falls back to sleep. She sleeps 23.9 hours a day; I am both grateful and jealous she's not awake to smell the antiseptic smells and see the needles they poke into the bottom of her feet every morning to check her blood gases. When I finally get out of the room, I rip the PPE off my face and body and take a deep breath. I whisper, *I will not vomit. I will not vomit. I will not vomit* like a mantra.

I am a vomiter. It's not that I am easily grossed out. I just have a low tolerance for neat shots of adrenaline straight to the gut. The thrill of skydiving made me vomit, as did all eight and a half of the car accidents I've been in. (Seven of which were not my fault.) I vomited when I sliced my finger on my mandolin, and when I got news of a college friend's passing. I am one to always locate the trash bin nearest my seat.

Pod 1 is circular with a nurse's station in the middle and patient rooms around the perimeter. Because of her aspergillus, Vivienne has been in an isolation room made for a single baby. They tell me it's to reduce her risk of infection, but I wonder if it's also to reduce our risk of infection. I decide not to do my own research on whether I, too, can catch a case of the "gilly." The patients in this pod are the tiniest babies born in this hospital. All but the two isolation rooms are double rooms separated by a washing station.

When I leave Vivienne's room after her wound care, I walk halfway around the pod and into the double room directly across from Vivienne's quarantine chamber. In this bigger room, without the confines of the face mask and the protective gown, I can breathe again, but only for a moment. One side of the room is empty, waiting for my baby to come out of isolation, but the other side has a slow cooker with a baby in it—also my baby.

Margot developed a white dot on her back, just a few days after Vivienne. We had already received Vivienne's positive biopsy results, so our medical team started medication before it got to the gaping wounds stage. I imagine a day when someone asks me how I can tell my identical twins apart, and I tell them a flesh-eating fungus took a bite of Vivienne's left butt cheek. Dark humor is my coping mechanism; no one is amused. I think the nurses and doctors worry about me. I worry about me too. At least we're all on the same page.

I sit in the chair next to Margot's isolette for a long while. Since the twins were born almost three weeks ago, my visits have been infrequent and short because I have not accepted these tiny babies hooked up to machines and living in slow cookers as my reality. If this is real, I am going to feel grief and desperation so intense I may die with my daughters. Just thinking about the severity of their condition gives me angina, so I don't come to this hospital often enough, and I don't sit in this chair for very long. I don't want to see my kids sustained by tubes down their throats and IV nutrition. I didn't want to see Vivienne's disfigured little body today.

No one really knows how much their life is going to change when they have their first baby, or, in my case, babies. You expect sleepless nights. You expect dirty diapers and maybe dirty bottles. Most of us do not expect the loss of identity and existential crisis that often ensues. I got none of what I expected when my daughters were born 17 weeks too soon, and I didn't get time or space or a mental health care professional to process what was going to happen before they were here in plastic boxes with machines breathing for them.

I was the one who told The Actual MD to save them. They are in this NICU because I wanted to give them a chance to live. I didn't realize how much they would suffer. I did this to them, and then I sat at home in my remote-controlled C-section chair, trying not to love them. When I told my family I didn't want to love my daughters because they were only going to die, I hadn't considered what would happen if they didn't die. I hadn't considered my kids would be warriors.

They are alive, but they exist somewhere in the middle of the harrowing spectrum between life and death. These babies—little girls smaller than dolls who can't even breathe for themselves—are fighting.

I am notorious for leaving tiny bits of crusted food on the side of dishes I've washed. When I don't have an editor, my work is littered with typos and comma splices. I never measure when I cook because it takes too long and it dirties extra dishes. Whatever the task, I just want it finished. I don't care if it's perfect. I am a destination person now stuck on a long and lamentable journey.

I have haphazardly put up walls to protect myself from getting hurt if this all goes to shit. I am avoiding vulnerability, and I am doing a shoddy job. My walls are crumbling; I am trying desperately to patch them. I avoid touching my kids. I spend only enough time in the NICU for the doctors and nurses to know these tiny twins have a mother, but never enough time to let myself feel the desperation waiting on the other side of my walls.

NOT WHAT I HAD IN MIND

I sit next to Margot's slow cooker replaying the events of the last three weeks. I have been trying so hard to avoid the pain of my daughters' impending deaths that I haven't given their lives very much thought. My chest tightens and vomit threatens to make an appearance. I debate calling the nurse to tell her I am having a heart attack, but they don't do adults here, so I sit with my desperation and my angina. *I am a mother. I am their mother.* Yet, I have been at home posting social media updates asking people on the internet to pray for them because if I were to pray for them—like really pray for them instead of just whispering wishes under my breath—I would have to acknowledge reality. If other people pray for them, well, their reality is between them and God.

The nurse taking care of Margot today is a tall, Swiss German woman with gentle eyes and a comforting smile. She looks about my age (well, my age before the twin pregnancy and traumatic birth got to me). She has wildly curly hair cut into a pixie. It is very cool. Her voice is grounding as she tells me babies whose parents are involved in their care have better survival rates. She is not shaming me, she is advocating for my daughters.

A 2018 study in the *Early Human Development Journal 44 January 8, 2020* entitled "Parent Participation in the Neonatal Intensive Care Unit" found parental participation in babies' NICU care improved developmental outcomes. This nurse has cared for Vivienne several times, but I've never seen her the way I do today. Today, I watch the way she pays close attention to Margot. I listen to the loving way she talks my daughter through a diaper change, and I see how she wants us to win. I feel the empathy in her voice when she explains ostomy output and new ventilator settings to me. I wish everyone in my life could understand the gravity of my situation the way she does. She is an advocate and a safe place in this storm. I ask The Advocate if the wound care nurse always comes around the same time. I tell her I would like to be here for Vivienne's wound care again tomorrow. I'm stepping into the arena.

Vulnerability is the state of being exposed to attack, be it physical or emotional. It is central to meaningful relationships. Vulnerability is a pilgrimage, not a destination. Vulnerability is a willingness to fight, even when you know you are likely to fail.

CHAPTER SIX

A Story for Sustenance

We tell stories to pass down traditions and to teach children how the world works. We tell stories to connect with each other and we tell stories to warn each other of looming danger. Stories help us make sense of the world, even when it least makes sense.

January 14, 2020

I am sitting next to Margot's slow cooker, searching for hope. Using my phone, I type *22-weeker twins* into search bars. Google yields nothing. Instagram yields two photos of micro babies like mine, except the babies in the photo are dead. They were denied medical intervention. Their mother held them while they died. I know little about medicine, but I know 100% of micro preemies denied care will not survive; this was not the story I was looking for.

I need hope. I need a story like ours, and I need it to have a happy ending. I broaden my social media search to *#22weeker* and find a few hundred photos. Turns out, people aren't using *#22weekertwins* because there aren't many; using *#22weeker* gives them more visibility.

I look through only a couple of photos before I see them. Not only do they look like happy, healthy babies, they are breathtaking. They are one-year-old twins with piercing eyes—one pair green, the other blue—dark, curly hair, smiling faces, and bows as big as their heads. I tap to follow their mother, Kayla Ibarra, and I scroll back to the beginning of their story.

Kayla has jet black hair and a pumpkin spice complexion. I am looking for connection and I wonder if she's Cuban, but as I dig deeper I find she's half black, a quarter Native American, and a quarter Irish. She's petite with a warm smile. I hardly know anything about her, but I know we will be friends.

Kayla walked into her local hospital 21 weeks and five days pregnant, thinking she might have a yeast infection. While she waited to be seen, her abdomen and her back cramped, symptoms she chalked up to the infection. Someone made a mistake when they checked her in, so she sat in the waiting room watching pregnant mothers come and go for hours. By the time the staff realized their error and started running tests, Kayla was sick with discomfort. When the tests came back negative for infection, she knew what was wrong.

"I'm in labor," she told the ultrasound technician.

"No, honey. Don't worry. You're not in labor. The doctor is going to check your cervix, though."

Kayla asked for permission to get off the table and move around to relieve her discomfort. The technician granted it and left the room. Kayla folded her upper body over the table to relieve the cramping, and a gush of water hit the ground. Seconds later, the technician re-entered the room. She looked down; her mouth fell agape.

"Now do you believe I'm in labor?" Kayla asked her.

Trauma has a weird way of making our brains omit certain details, while amplifying others. My memories of the last month look like broad paint strokes with little pockets of microscopic details. I remember the sound and sensation of my water breaking and The Actual MD squatting down to my level to ask me what I wanted to do with Vivienne. But the two days that followed blend into each other. As I piece together Kayla's story from short videos and photographs, I notice the details her brain has fixated on, and I see the broad strokes where one color turns to another, but it's hard to tell exactly where or how.

One minute Kayla was in the ultrasound room standing in a pool of her daughters' amniotic fluid; the next she was being rolled into an elevator.

"What will happen to my daughters?" She asked the nurse wheeling her.

"I'm sorry. Your babies will be born today and they will die." The nurse responded.

Even the most anxious mother doesn't expect to find herself in labor at 21 weeks and five days gestation. We may type our biggest fears into search engines, but we don't research the hospitals, medications, and protocols that can save us if our fears come true. Kayla was at a hospital that wouldn't treat her babies because she had not reached viability—which, they told her was 24 weeks. She had no reason to know the line of viability changed depending on where you are and who you talk to. She could have accepted what they told her; that's what I think I would have done. But something in her (something she and I both call God) told her to fight for her daughters.

At 22 weeks gestation, a mother can decide to let her baby die, but only doctors and hospital policy makers decide if that same baby gets a chance to live. Not only is the line of viability a moving target (depending on the hospital you go to and the doctor you get), but gestational age is an estimate. Unless a baby is conceived via in vitro fertilization, there is no way to know exactly when an egg is fertilized. An egg can be fertilized shortly after intercourse, but there have been cases where it appears to have taken five full days. Ultrasound measurements are not always accurate either, adding yet another confounding factor. A mother might be denied intervention at 22 weeks and 6 days, but granted intervention the very next day. A single day can be the difference between life and death, and that day may be nothing more than a margin of error. Most people don't know any of this until it's too late—until they are at a hospital with a high-risk obstetrician telling them they can't help unless they can stay pregnant for another two days. If my girls had kept growing inside me and had made it through most of the third trimester, I may never have learned the word *periviable*. I would not know there are right places and wrong places to have a premature baby.

The on-call OB assigned to Kayla's case didn't even feign hope. She pushed Kayla to expedite her labor. Pitocin would speed up her contractions; it would bring the twins into the world sooner. She could get this nightmare over with, if she would just agree. She refused the Pitocin. The physician refused to do anymore ultrasounds, warning her she need not grow attached to these babies who would surely die.

The morphine they gave Kayla for her pain brought her labor to a halt, buying her a bit of time, but not enough. The hospital staff tried and failed again to expedite Kayla's labor. Again, she refused. She was adamant that her babies were to stay exactly where they were until an act of God brought them into the world. The medical team stopped pushing her to consent to Pitocin. They told her if she could make it to 24 weeks, they would transfer her to a hospital with a better-equipped NICU.

Baby A's feet were already visible in Kayla's birth canal. There was no chance of making it to 24 weeks. For four days, Kayla asked every doctor and nurse she saw for a transfer to a hospital that would save her babies. They grew so tired of her demands and of her refusal to speed up her labor that they stopped checking on her as often as they should have. By the time her doctor in shining armor arrived, Kayla had pneumonia and was in active labor again.

"Kayla, I read your chart, and I know your desire is to save these babies. I'm going to call around to level 3 and 4 NICUs and see if anyone is willing to take you," the doctor told her.

In piecing together Kayla's story, I understand for the first time that where a baby is born is a matter of life and death for babies like mine. A doctor may squander any chance of life if he or she hasn't read the data from a hospital like the University of Iowa. At Iowa, most 22-weekers survive. In 2000, Dr. Edward Bell started the Tiniest Babies Registry at the University of Iowa tracking babies born weighing less than 14 ounces. In October

2019, Bell and his colleagues used that data to publish a paper in the Journal of Pediatrics. Of 255 babies born between 22 and 23 weeks gestation, survival to hospital discharge was 78%. At 18-22 months (adjusted for prematurity), 60% of survivors had no or mild neurodevelopmental impairments. These outcomes are what's possible when babies are born in a place that's fighting for them.

Most hospitals are still operating on the premise that babies born before 24 weeks can't survive. Most hospitals are not transferring patients like Kayla to a hospital with better outcomes for micro preemies. Doctors under the impression that most 22-weekers die are not even willing to make a 15-minute phone call, let alone fight for a 22-weeker's life.

Kayla's story makes me wonder: Where would I be right now if I didn't live five minutes away from the best NICU in the state of Florida? Would I have had the wherewithal to fight? Would I have even known I could fight? I am grateful I won't ever learn the answers to these questions because I was in the right place at the right time. I'm grateful Kayla had all the determination I may not have had.

Kayla's doctor came back just fifteen minutes later with news that two hospitals were willing to take her and provide medical intervention for her daughters. That "yes" changed the course of Kayla's life. Still in labor, they loaded her into an ambulance to London, Ontario.

Even at this new hospital that had willingly accepted Kayla as a transfer, knowing she was in active labor with 22-weeker twins, she was pressured one last time to let her daughters go. They were willing to grant her the medical intervention she wanted, but they were perpetuating the narrative that 22-weekers don't survive. She rejected their narrative.

Luna and Ema came into this world at 22 weeks and 2 days gestation, weighing less than one pound each. They spent months with a ventilator breathing for them. They fought fungal infections and had tiny holes in their hearts. They spent four months in the NICU, coming home two weeks before their due date.

This is the happiest ending I could have hoped to find, and I'm crying now. They are strange tears, both joyful and heartbroken, inspired and devastated. How can someone be strong enough to fight for something they barely understand during such trauma? Kayla is a warrior and her daughters are my most tangible hope right now. I send her a message: *Every time I need to remember there is hope and God can make a way, I will scroll through the photos of your daughters. Thank you for sharing your story.*

Gratitude is not a word I would use to describe the way I feel about our circumstances, but I am glad for what I know now about viability and periviability. I am living a nightmare, but I have a feeling this is not in vain. Someday, I will be a supporter of hospitals that fight for babies like mine. Someday, our story is going to mean something to someone. It's going to give a scared mother hope or help a pregnant woman choose the right hospital. One day, I will be someone's Kayla.

As I scroll, I see Kayla is launching TwentyTwo Matters, an organization dedicated to getting the word out that 22-weekers are not only viable, but they can thrive. She has been creating a map of hospitals that will intervene at 22 weeks. She and her co-founder advocate for mothers in extremely premature labor to get the medical care they want for their babies. Over the next few years, our friendship and her organization will grow. She will advocate for babies when their mothers are overwhelmed by fear and grief. By the time her daughters are four years old, TwentyTwo Matters will have over 15,400 members, and hospitals around the world will know Kayla, Luna, and Ema.

There is a fine line between delusion and hope, but I'm not delusional. I know the bowel perforations and the aspergillus are working against my daughters. I know there is a broad gray area between surviving and living a perfectly typical life alongside your peers. I know the internet has more stories about 22-weekers who die than 22-weekers who thrive, but if I am to keep showing up here, I have to hope for a story like Kayla's.

Stories are what we look for and cling to when we most need hope and connection. From the holy miracles found in the pages of the Bible to the human miracle of those who step up in the face of tragedy, our hearts long for hope and our brains want to make sense of suffering by giving it a beginning, middle, and end. The accounts of those who came before us are a reminder of the beauty that can come from what was once only ashes.

CHAPTER SEVEN

Hold Your comments, Not My Daughters

January 9, 2020

Vivienne is unwell. Because of her aspergillus infection, she is still in the isolation room across the pod from Margot. She is on maximum respiratory support and an epinephrine drip. Epi, as it's commonly called, is a vasopressor. Pressors, another nickname, narrow blood vessels to increase blood pressure. Vivienne's low blood pressure could be a sign of infection, especially when combined with the deterioration of her respiratory status. They cultured her blood for infection last night, but no bacteria has grown yet. The doctors suspect sepsis. Normally, they want to know exactly what strain of bacteria is causing an infection before they treat it.

A tall, tan neonatalogist with a head of salt and pepper hair and a northern accent is rounding today. His word choice and the tone of his voice radiate compassion. He seems like the kind of man I would choose as my daughters' godfather, if I were Catholic. The Godfather says they can't wait any longer for bacteria to grow on Vivienne's blood culture. He orders antibiotics to get ahead of the infection and tells the nurse to start them right away. I know from my prime time TV medical drama education that sepsis is life-threatening.

There are days when I think of all the people praying for my daughters and I am convinced God could not possibly ignore so many of his people begging for their lives. Today is not one of those days.

I have been sitting next to the slow cookers all day. I alternate between babies. I sanitize my cracked hands half a dozen times before I open the portals into their little worlds and ever-so-gently cup their heads. I whisper prayers of desperation, and I think about how I am going to raise Margot without Vivienne. How will I get up and pour a cup of coffee and put oatmeal on the stove for Margot without grieving the identical little girl who should be standing next to her?

Vivienne and Margot are monochorionic diamniotic twins, commonly referred to as mo/di or mono/di twins. This means they shared a placenta, the organ that develops in pregnancy to sustain a baby's life, but they had separate amniotic sacs. Mono/di twins don't run in families. They happen spontaneously—like a glitch in the matrix—when one egg and one sperm join together and the fertilized egg splits into two after conception.

For a moment in time, my daughters were one. Then, they shared a womb, and they shared their source of nutrients and oxygen. I have heard dozens of times that twins have an other-worldly bond. I don't know how Margot could live her whole life disconnected from the part of herself that didn't get to live. This hypothetical future should make me sad, but I don't want my daughters to sense through the plastic of their slow cookers that I've lost hope, so I shove my thoughts and feelings deep inside where it's dark and fireproof.

My mom and my mother-in-law sit in solidarity with me. They are holding onto their composure for my sake, and if they knew the dark and twisty depths of my mind, everyone's composure would surely be lost. They know they can't make me feel better, but that doesn't stop them from wanting to. I imagine they'd like to make themselves feel better too, which I have to assume is why my mother-in-law has allowed herself to dream of a day when she might hold her granddaughters. That *would* be a happier day than this one, and the thought of such a day compels her to say aloud that she can't wait to hold them. I feign a smile because I know she is pure; she would never want to hurt anyone—especially not me—but this unlocks the fireproof safe where I've been shoving my feelings.

I excuse myself. I walk out of Pod 1 and down the hallway past the hand-washing stations. I pass the milk ladies on my right, acknowledging them with a nod, and I press the button to exit the NICU. I silently praise the Lord when I reach for the restroom door and it's unoccupied. I step in, lock the door behind me, and slide down the door onto the bathroom floor. With my face in my hands, my tears trickle like a faucet that drips if you don't turn it off just right.

Everyone knows I'm grieving, and it makes them uneasy. Internally, I'm raging, but on the outside I am a mournful mother. Most people back away from my sadness slowly; others try to hide the parts of their lives they fear might remind me of my grief. People leave their kids at home or in the car when they drop off dinner to us, like maybe I won't remember they have kids so I won't think of my own daughters being kept alive with IVs, ventilators, and vasopressors.

There are the people who ignore grief and opt to pretend to understand how God works. They tell themselves he is good; therefore, my daughters will be OK. They let themselves dream of a future in which they might kiss and cuddle my daughters without fear that germs will kill them. Anything resembling normalcy threatens to destroy the place where I hide my pain. I smile and nod when friends and family tell me they can't wait to meet the babies. Afterwards, I rage at Jerod, as though he should fix humanity. He should make people more sensitive.

The first time I saw Vivienne, I was still pregnant with Margot. I tried not to cry, for fear of stressing Margot. Vivienne's skin was translucent. Her underdeveloped eyes were covered with the world's tiniest knitted hat to protect them from the light. She looked just like I imagined a fetus would look. Her ears weren't fully formed and her fingers were long, skinny, and unrealistic—like fingers you would find on a plastic doll. I thought she was beautiful. Though, objectively, she was not. That day, I let the salty water fall down my face as I understood the etymology of motherhood. Motherhood is rooted in believing the very best about our children. We believe they are kind, capable, and beautiful, even when it's a far stretch. The nurse noticed my tears and told me to stay hopeful. "Don't cry," she said. "They can sense it."

I didn't want my daughters to sense my sadness, so I asked for my wheelchair, and my nurse accompanied me back to my room on the labor and delivery floor. I ran my fingers up my cheeks, as if to squeegee the tears back inside. I locked my feelings away that day. But even a fireproof safe cannot withstand an explosive that detonates from within.

Here I am, nearly a month after my daughters' births, still trying to mitigate the threat of implosion. I will not survive this, and it's not because my mother-in-law is talking about holding my daughters. It's because I am a mother who's never held her daughters, and I don't know if I ever will.

Margot is living and Vivienne is trying not to die; yet I am the one crying into my hands on a hospital restroom floor. I wash my face. I look in the mirror, and I tell myself I am the mother. *Pull yourself together. Scrub to your elbows and get back to this messed up version of motherhood you've been dealt.*

I know we have to allow ourselves to *feel* grief in order to move through it. We cannot hide our most intense feelings in dark, locked corners of our hearts because they will find their way out and they will hurt people. But for now I cannot allow myself to fall apart. If my daughters live, I need to remember everything that happens. I need to know how their bodies work—or don't. I have to know that they will have piccolos occluding their patent ductus arteriosis. I have to keep straight that Vivienne has an ileostomy and Margot has a jejeunostomy. In an emergency, I may have to recall Margot's sensitive vasovagal response. I cannot forget Margot has cholestasis and some medications may not be appropriate for her. If I am to remember all of this—if I am to make sure that every doctor who treats my kids has the whole picture—I cannot fall apart now. I have to wait until they are OK, or until they are dead.

I dry my face. I walk back into the NICU. I scrub again and again and again, and I make my way back to the double room with just one baby in it. My mother-in-law had to leave, and I am grateful she is not here to see my puffy eyes and runny nose. I am grateful my very big feelings are locked away again when The Real Life Arizona Robbins almost bounces into the room to ask me if I'm going to hold Margot today. She says it so casually because, for a second, she forgot I've never held Margot. I pause long enough for her to realize this, and she is delighted. "Oh my gosh," she says. "Today is the day. How long will you be here? Can you wait a bit? I'll rally the troops."

On my first solo trip to the NICU after I was discharged, a young blonde with a 24-weeker baby boy greeted me at the hand washing station. She had been a NICU mom for 42 days. She was the first person to tell me the NICU is a rollercoaster. I've heard it at least two dozen times since then, and I am well acquainted with the rollercoaster. I have been riding it for 25 days, but it's never escalated quite so quickly. I am going to hold my daughter today. In a matter of minutes, I've gone from crying on the restroom floor to the highlight of my mothering career. I am here for the ride. The wait feels so long. I am certain my hair has grown gray and I have developed crow's feet. But then, right before I drop dead of old age, The Real Arizona arrives with the troops.

While Margot is in better shape than her sister, there is still a mess of wires attached to machines that are keeping her alive. Two nurses and two respiratory therapists agree it's best for Margot to go straight from her slow cooker to my chest, rather than from the cooker to the nurse's arms to my chest. They pull the curtain closed. I slip a hospital gown on backward so I can bring my daughter to my bare skin when it's time. They open the side of the isolette like a DeLorean, and now we're doing this.

Four weeks post C-section, I have zero core strength in my exhausted and broken body. I dig deep for the sturdiness to perform this delicate operation. I slide my hands under my one-and-a-half-pound daughter. A respiratory therapist secures the endotracheal tube in Margot's mouth between her gloved fingers. A nurse secures her PICC line, an almost-central IV feeding her total parenteral nutrition and medicating her with amphotericin, caffeine, hydrocortisone, and whatever else she needs to keep her alive today. I look at the nurse and then the respiratory therapist, awaiting the go-ahead to bring my daughter to my bare chest.

Someone says it's time. I am shaking from the exertion of moving her so slowly while trying not to cry. The foot and a half between her box and my chest seems as wide as the Capertee Valley, but 83 seconds later Margot Midiam is safely on my chest. But this is only half our journey. There is another foot and a half between us and the sterile blue chair where we will get to know each other. As anyone who has ever had their gut sliced open knows, one does not simply sit down after such an insult to the abdomen. I have to use my arms to lower myself gently, but my arms are protecting the tiniest treasure. This is why I need five people to help me hold my second-born daughter today.

With a human support system under each arm and the littlest baby held gingerly, yet securely, to my chest, her own support crew keeping her life-sustaining tubes in place, we make it to the blue chair. I breathe and I cry. My tears are dripping on Margot, and I wonder if that's OK. I notice how her whole body fits between my chin and my collarbone. She is insubstantial; yet she is a force. Her forearms are smaller than my pinky fingers. No one else will ever comprehend how impossibly tiny my daughters are. She smells sterile, and I can feel her skin sticking to mine. She knows she is home. She falls fast asleep. Her vitals are perfect. This is perfect.

I hold her for hours, until my bladder and my boobs are full, and then we do the whole dance in reverse. My human support system helps me put my baby back into her slow cooker. When we are finished, The Real Arizona drops in to inform me that Vivienne is improving. The Godfather's call to start antibiotics in anticipation of sepsis saved her life. They successfully weaned her respiratory support. They plan on weaning the pressors tomorrow morning. I crack open my safe because I want to let myself feel all of this: the fear, the sorrow, the helplessness, and the song of joy playing over it all right now.

CHAPTER EIGHT

An All-encompassing Disease For The People

Some of us go through life relaxed—unchecked boxes and unmade beds are just a part of life. Some of us are more high-strung—clenching steering wheels when the drive-thru takes a minute too long and throwing our hands up in exasperation at life's little inconveniences. But we all have our thresholds; we all have our breaking points. When it comes to trauma, most people can withstand much more than they think they can. There are limits, though. The heart can only take so much before it's at capacity.

March 15, 2020

Pandemic comes from the Greek root words *pan* meaning all-encompassing and *demotic* which denotes a belonging to the people. My father, anticipating the collapse of the world as we know it, has been keeping us abreast of the latest news on the impending pandemic since December. Whenever he mentioned it, I would politely nod. I told myself I would think about the coronavirus if it got here. A woman can only handle so much!

Today, the World Health Organization acknowledged COVID-19 as a global pandemic, and I'm worrying about it a lot. My mom is sitting in the twins' hospital room with me, as she has every day for the last three months. The nurse manager comes in with a memo: as of today, the only visitors allowed in the NICU are parents, and only one parent can come in at a time. There have been rumors of this for a week. This is not a surprise as much as it is a blow to the gut. And I have questions. *We have two babies. Shouldn't each baby get two visitors? Shouldn't the rules be different for those of us who are permanent fixtures here? How does my crumbling mental health factor in here?*

She tells me she will see what she can do, and I believe her because my parents are the most involved parents this NICU has ever seen. My father has not missed a day of rounds in 91 days. My mother has spent nearly a thousand hours sitting next to slow cookers, reading "Winny de Puh" to my tiny girls.

The nurse manager comes back a couple of hours later with a compromise. Jerod and I can both be in the NICU at the same time, but my parents have to go until we can flatten the curve. She and I both know this is a script she's been sent to deliver because people don't say "flatten the curve" in real life. I've spent 91 days in the NICU and I get a script just like everyone else.

Our circumstances feel uniquely tragic, like there should be an exception to the rules for us, but isn't that the case for every family here? We all find ourselves stuck in an intensive care unit with vulnerable babies in the middle of a global health crisis. We're all being stripped of the little support we have. We are all in this together, but none of us are looking around long enough to realize it. Our desperation is blinding.

I knew a highly contagious respiratory virus was going to be critical on a unit full of immunocompromised kids with lung disease. I figured hospital politics would prevent anyone from bending the rules, even for their favorite patients, but this is still sad and sobering.

I have spent so much time in this hospital that I know more about our nurses than I know about some of my oldest friends. I know The Advocate hasn't been able to get pregnant and is considering fertility treatments. I know The Fabulous One with the long black hair is not coming back to work after her wedding. I know their spiritual beliefs and their marital statuses. They feel like family, and family would make an exception for my parents. But they aren't the ones making these decisions. They work for an organization that is trying to make the best call for everyone.

Since the girls were born at Christmastime, people were extra generous. In the days between Christmas and New Year's Day, I got hundreds of texts. Visitors came daily with gift cards and dinner. Our friends held prayer vigils in our front yard and in the hospital lobby. But when January came, they all went back to work, and I stayed locked in this hospital. My trauma is not their trauma; my little girls are not their little girls.

There are a few exceptions, the rare friend still reaching out all these months later to ask if she can bring me coffee and take a walk with me around the hospital. There are people texting and emailing me to ask how they can pray specifically over the parts of my daughters' bodies that most need healing. They are often the people I least expect, people I hardly knew before my daughters came too soon. For the most part, though, the world has moved on and I am standing still. And now, the people who have been standing with me—the ones who have been holding me up—have to go.

When we first got here, we filled out paperwork so the nurses would know Jerod and I were the only people allowed to hold Vivienne and Margot. At that time, we weren't even allowed to hold them, so it seemed incomprehensible to let our parents or siblings hold them. Today, I asked the nurses if we can ignore the paperwork. I want my parents to hold their granddaughters until the nurse manager kicks them out. I want my parents to have a bit of joy on this very sad day.

There are still four weeks between now and when the girls should have been born, but they have graduated from slow cookers to open warmers—a miniature crib with an overhead heater like what you might sit under at a hair salon. My father still finds my daughters so very breakable. He's hesitant to touch them, let alone pick them up, but I insist. There are significantly fewer tubes than there were two months ago when I first held my daughters. They are nearly four times heavier and—at least for today—neither of them is intubated.

The babies are stable, but surgery is imminent. Outcomes are never guaranteed. I cannot know whether my parents and my daughters will ever see each other again. My dad picks up Vivienne; the room is loaded with sorrow and delight at the same time. He stands next to her bed and holds her for just a few minutes, whispering a song, and—because he is an honorable and just *abuelo*—he makes his way over to Margot's warmer and performs the ritual again before saying his goodbye.

My mother pulls the blue chair next to Vivienne's warmer. The Advocate places the baby in her arms. I sit across the room in an identical blue chair with an identical baby in my arms. For hours, we spontaneously burst into laughter and then into tears because this is both lovely and ridiculous. When the nurse manager peeks into the room, we are still holding the babies, and I know she's here to call it a day—a last day. My mom cries as she sets Vivienne back in her bed and, as if she knows the world is not right, Vivienne cries too. This makes me cry. Margot, feeling left out, begins to whimper. It doesn't matter that everyone is crying, my mom has to go and I am alone because it's hospital policy.

I am a dawn patroller. Most days I wake up before everyone else in the neighborhood so I can be alone with my thoughts and my 40 ounces of coffee. I think more clearly and learn faster when the world is quiet. I am not just used to being alone, I relish solitude. But being alone in this NICU, while my husband works and my parents have been asked to leave, is lonely. With all the emotions I'm carrying, lonely is too heavy a burden to add. With nowhere to go and no one to talk to, I venture into my psyche unaccompanied.

Why are we here? Why would a good God create the world only for evil to enter it? What is the point of living when the people you love could die? Can suffering kill you? Is there a point at which needle pokes, and breathing tubes, and ostomy bags, and edema, and breast pumps, and retinopathy of prematurity, and the novel coronavirus, and the arctic temperatures in this hospital will end me?

Jerod started a new job last month. The company is gracious about our situation, but if he doesn't work, he doesn't get paid. He is doing everything he can to be here for the three of us, but he can't live in this NICU like I do. Without him and my parents here, I don't think I can do this. The weight of the situation will break me without their support.

My father has been anticipating the collapse of the world by way of the novel coronavirus, but maybe we all should have been anticipating my collapse.

PART 2: NOTHING'S FINE; I'M TORN

CHAPTER NINE

Bypassing Delight

Beginnings are exciting. We love the flutter of initial attraction. The novelty of a new project or a new job drives us to show up—to pursue, to work, to create. Even when beginnings are terrifying, we enter into stories and seasons of life with a naïveté that allows us to hope and dream. We are eager to find out what happens next. At the beginning of a tragedy, people wrap themselves around the suffering party. They send blankets and bring casseroles. They wait with bated breath. But as we inch toward the middle, the support wavers and the meal train comes to a grinding halt.

Endings are, at the very least, conclusive. At their best, they make us believe in rainbows, and butterflies, and love. At their worst, we may be left broken-hearted, but at least we have permission to process our grief and move on—something the middle would never allow.

We call it the messy middle, which sounds cute, but there is nothing cute about it, is there? The middle is the part where we are actively drowning or starving or stewing over an unanswered text message. The middle is a steaming pile of produce scraps and dirty diapers on the asphalt at 3 p.m. in Florida…in *July*!

We talk about the value of a journey, but it's one thing to take a Euro trip and another thing entirely to live in hospital hell. Journeys twist and turn and complicate our lives. They are riddled with uncertainty. They breed anxiety. The middle represents a total loss of control. And maybe some of us can surrender to God or fate, but is that really our preference? Or, if given the chance, would we peek at the end of the story? We don't want messy middles. We want casseroles and happily ever afters.

March 17, 2020

Reanastomosis is a reuniting of a divided vessel, specifically by way of surgery. In Latin, when *an* precedes a vowel, it indicates something is in place or renewed. *Stoma* is a small opening in a body, an orifice. It comes from Greek and it means mouthpiece, which indicates an inlet or an outlet. The pieces of my daughters' intestines that stick out through the holes in their abdomens are called ostomies, or sometimes just stomas. It's an outlet for their stool, it's an outlet Vivienne won't have anymore after today, but Margot still will.

For the last three months, part of their intestines have been sticking out from holes in their bellies so they can poop. The other part of their intestines are in a little bag inside their bodies. Hopefully, the part of the intestines in the little bag has spent the last three months healing, and when they open them up they will find beautiful, perfused bowel that can be stitched to the rest of their guts. It's wild how you can go from hoping your babies will have your hair and their father's eyes to hoping for good blood flow to their intestines.

It's hard to remember a time before perfused intestines were my greatest hope. Three months ago I didn't know anything about stomas or positive expiratory end pressure. Three months ago, my naïveté protected me, but now I know too much.

Today, I understand Vivienne will have her ostomy reversed, or reanastomosed. They will connect her ileum, the last section of the small intestine, to her ileocecal valve, which is the sphincter that separates the small and large intestines. The ileocecal valve is a big deal. We need it to be intact when they open her or we're facing a lifetime of diarrhea and bacterial contamination from the colon to the small intestine. When Vivienne is all connected, she will poop in a diaper like a typical baby. If not for the four-inch scar across her belly, no one will ever know she spent the first three months of her life shitting into a bag.

Margot is more complicated. Behemoth Hands told us there was a strong possibility she would come home with an ostomy bag. We hoped he was wrong. Even The Possibility Doctor, The Actual MD, and The Real Life Arizona Robbins were hopeful. But when they did her pre-operative scans, they found a micro colon, too tiny to do its job. Since her colon has been unused, it hasn't grown with the rest of her. Behemoth Hands explains he will connect her jejunum, which is currently a stoma sticking out of her belly, to the ileum and create an ileostomy so she can use more of her digestive tract to absorb her nutrients. In a year, if the colon has grown, they will put her back together.

He says *if* the colon has grown, and I feel like the oxygen has been vacuumed from the room. Lately, I walk into this NICU full of gratitude that my daughters are alive and we can see a path home, but right now I am disappointed. I've thought about what it would be like to have one daughter live and one daughter die, but I had not considered what it would be like to take one daughter home whole and another still in need of assembly, her insides on the outside. How do I parent twins with different abilities? How do I not feel sorry for Margot? In my sorrow, how do I make her feel like her sister is her equal when their bodies will work so differently? I know I am going to mess them up, and I'm overwhelmed.

In addition to Margot's partial reanastomosis, Behemoth Hands will place a gastrostomy tube in her stomach so we can feed her continuously and very slowly through this tube. Feeding her this way won't overtax her delicate digestive system; in theory, it should help her absorb more nutrients.

A gastrostomy tube (g-tube for short) is not unlike the air valve on a beach ball, except instead of pushing air into a plastic ball, this valve allows you to push saline into a tiny, silicone balloon that's hollow through the middle. It is a donut-shaped balloon attached to a plastic cap that has two valves. One of the valves goes into the balloon, the other valve goes through the donut hole and into the stomach. When the balloon is deflated, it is essentially a thick pin you can stick through the hole in the abdomen all the way into the stomach. You then use a plastic syringe in the valve that goes directly to the ballon to fill the balloon with saline. The filled balloon, now in the stomach, keeps the g-tube button in place so it lays flat on the belly. The button has a flap, just like the valve on the beach ball. The flap gives access to the tube that goes through the donut hole and into the belly. You can pump medication through this valve with a syringe or you can hook up a pump to push breast milk, formula, or puréed food through the valve into the baby. It's a medical marvel that bypasses the mouth. It bypasses the tastebuds. It bypasses delight.

The g-tube is supposed to improve nutrient absorption, but it's also an insurance policy for feeding issues. While Margot was the first of my daughters to breathe without a ventilator, she hasn't been able to stay off the ventilator for more than a week at a time. In contrast, Vivienne took longer to come off the vent, but the girl never looked back. Kids who are on ventilators for a long time often develop oral aversions. The textures and flavors of milk and first foods disgust them; they won't eat by mouth. This is not the kind of thing I can parent my way out of with admonitions about how hungry she'll be later if she doesn't eat dinner. It could take years of g-tube feeds and feeding therapy to get my daughter to eat.

I love food. I love to plan meals. I love the layering of flavors. The smell of simmering curry is always wafting out of our house into the neighbors' yards. There is always a sourdough starter on my counter feasting on fresh flour, waiting to be turned into bread. Cooking is in my DNA. My father comes alive as he turns disparate ingredients into a giant paella or a mushroom risotto. He can spend all afternoon in the kitchen listening to an audiobook and making culinary art. I am unintimidated by recipes with dozens and dozens of ingredients and a trillion steps. My love of food is not just about the pleasure of hot and crispy garlic fresh off my stove, it's about the beauty of this gift from God.

Food sustains us, *and* it can delight us. Food is a full-body sensory experience. You can see it, smell it, taste it, and even hear it sizzling on a grill or simmering in a Dutch oven. A nostalgic meal can unearth parts of our memory we thought were long gone. Plates piled with quinoa, roasted broccoli, and chickpeas topped with homemade ginger miso dressing can nourish and heal a body. It is not accidental that food is beautiful, delicious, healing, and creative. It's divine, and I don't know when, or if, Margot will ever experience my favorite gift from God.

I am not a parenting expert. I am hardly a parent at all, seeing as how I've never even been unsupervised with my three-month-old daughters, but I know you have to choose your battles as a parent. No matter how much I want my kids to have the best of everything, I am just one person with limited resources. When I found out I was pregnant, I spent a good, long time pondering the parenting hills I would die on. What really matters to me is that my daughters experience God-inspired wonder. As a writer, I want desperately for them to feel the magic and beauty of language deep in their souls. And I want to cultivate an appreciation for food—from Indian curries, and Cuban black beans, to colorful and flavorful combinations even I haven't tasted yet. It is not the news of micro colon that makes me come apart at my loosely woven seams. It's the g-tube. It's the bypassing of delight.

I had plans to sustain my daughters on vegetables grown in my backyard and on local farms. I dreamt of raising them on ancient grains like amaranth, barley, farro, and sorghum drenched in homemade sauces. I thought I would breastfeed until they were at least 23-years-old. I hoped they would be the first modern Americans to make it to adulthood without consuming preservatives and added sugar, and now I'm researching the ingredients in the formula I'll be funneling into Margot's g-tube and realizing they won't even make it out of the hospital without consuming preservatives and added sugars.

My disappointment over my broken dreams of motherhood are not a clinical reason for pause, so the medicine must go on. Vivienne goes to surgery and comes back whole. Margot goes to surgery; we wait and wait, my insides in knots all the while. The hospital uses a mobile application called *Ease* to send us HIPAA-compliant updates on surgery. The updates let us know when they started and that surgery is progressing as planned, but this is not enough to put us at ease. (Oh the irony!)

I watch parents come and go. From the outside, we all look so well-adjusted—nothing like people whose children are in an operating room somewhere anesthetized, their bodies cut open. Margot has been in the OR more than twice as long as Vivienne when the app rings with an alert. *Surgery went well. Closing now.*

I was holding onto hope for a different outcome until the last minute. When they roll her back into the room and I see her new stoma, a few inches below where the old stoma was, I am gutted. I wanted a different kind of miracle. I wanted more than just a living, breathing daughter with a fully functional brain. Maybe I wanted too much. Just above and to the right of the new stoma is a white g-tube button. I look at it for a long time. My daughter has overcome more in her three months of life than most people overcome in a lifetime. A piece of plastic will not be what holds her back. If anything, this piece of plastic will propel her forward.

CHAPTER TEN

A Mother Cut in Half

April, 28, 2020

Just a couple of weeks after the girls' surgeries, Vivienne was weaned off supplemental oxygen. I took a walk around Pod 1 holding my daughter, not a single tube attached to her five-pound frame. Vivienne didn't belong in Pod 1 anymore. She was surrounded by the tiniest, sickest babies, but she is none of those things. When a room became available on the 11th floor of the hospital, the level II NICU, they offered it to us. We moved to the land of babies who just need to feed and grow.

I've been living on the 11th floor of Orlando Health Winnie Palmer Hospital for Women and Babies for five weeks now. Our private room has a shower and a sofa bed. While she did have to go back on supplemental oxygen when she started feeding by mouth, I can pick up Vivienne unsupervised—and whenever I want! I feed her—sometimes the breast, sometimes the bottle — like a regular mom with a healthy baby.

A few days ago, the medical director of the NICU came to see us. While we have been in the NICU for nearly half a year, we don't know him the way we know The Possibility Doctor, The Real Life Arizona Robbins, and The Actual MD. The Medical Director seemed happy when he walked in. This struck me because I know him to be an even-tempered man, showing little emotion. He looked at wide-eyed Vivienne as she kicked her feet and he said to me, "If she continues to gain weight over the next two days, she can go home Tuesday." I looked at my phone to see that it was Friday. In four days' time, Vivienne Nora Freeland, the first of her name, could be home instead of in a hospital.

Months ago, I decided not to let myself think about going home. I accepted the neonatal intensive care unit as my new life. Since we moved to the 11th floor, I haven't left the hospital. The nurses make me go downstairs to get an updated name tag every day for security reasons, but I eat here and I shower here, and suddenly this doctor with the power to release my daughter into my care tells me I'll be taking her home. Initially, I was confused because this is my home. My other daughter lives just eight floors down, and I cannot reconcile how my two babies could live in separate places when I can only be in one place at a time. Salt water started streaming down my face and my sinuses filled with mucus. This nice man with a very important job probably thought it was a happy cry because he said, "Oh, has no one talked to you about discharge?" He smiled, gave me a pat on the shoulder, and congratulated me, but it was not a happy cry. It was the cry of a mother faced with an impossible choice.

There is a story in the Old Testament of two mothers. They are prostitutes who live in the same house and who both have baby boys. One of the baby boys dies, and each mother claims the surviving child is hers. They bring their dispute before King Solomon. He calls for a sword and declares his intention to cut the baby in half, giving each mother half a baby boy. While this king is renowned in the Bible for his wisdom, I can't help but think his approach is inappropriate in the face of two mothers, one grieving and the other terrified. I'd like to think he wasn't really going to cut the baby in half, but the Old Testament often reads like *Game of Thrones*, so who knows. Regardless, the barbaric threat works. The baby's actual mother loves him enough to let him go if it means he gets to live. She begs the king not to kill the baby; she pleads with him to give the boy to the false mother. The false mother, grieving the loss of her baby, is so desperate she agrees to Solomon's savage solution. If she can't have a whole baby, no one else can either. The depths of the real mother's love reveals everything the king needs to know. A mother willing to be separated from her baby, rather than seeing him cut in half, is a real mother. This is how King Solomon made his decision and narrowly avoided going down in history as The Baby Slayer.

I am the *real* mom in the story of King Soloman's judgment. Instead of one baby cut in half, I am one mother cut in half by two babies, and, for the foreseeable future, I can only choose one.

Today is Vivienne's Discharge Day. I go downstairs to sit by Margot whose belly is swollen. After surgery, her incision became infected, and now she's not passing stool. Our doctors are monitoring her closely for a potential bowel obstruction. I snuggle my cheek next to hers and

I let my tears run down her face. This is the hardest day. This is harder than deciding on the DNR. This is harder than waiting for the results of potentially fatal surgeries. This is harder than the day I held my breath as I waited for the neurosonogram results. The longer I know them, the more I love them. The more I love them, the more intense the disappointment.

The Possibility Doctor and The Actual MD come by. They are overjoyed one of my daughters is going home. One Freeland twin has defied all odds, and that's better than what they expected. The enthusiasm fades as they note my sadness. I don't have to explain. Margot's bloated little body tells them everything they need to know. They acknowledge my plight with solemn nods. The Actual MD gives me a hug and I cry into his scrubs.

I am a long-distance runner. Obviously, I have not laced up my shoes in quite some time, but when I train for a big race, I increase my mileage every Saturday. Three to four miles feels doable. Even five to six miles doesn't seem so bad, but every season when it's time to do that first double-digit run, I wake up anxious that I won't make it. I always do, though. The next Saturday, when I have to run 11 miles, my heart flutters and I am certain this run will be the one where I simply cannot go on. This goes on every weekend for five to seven weeks. On race days, I stand at the start line and then I put one foot in front of the other for 69,168 feet. After what feels like 40 years in the desert (but was really just two hours in the Florida sun), I cross the finish line. It doesn't matter how many times I do this dance. I am always emotional when I cross.

NOT WHAT I HAD IN MIND

Seeing my kids suffer and suffering alongside them does not make me different from most mothers. It makes me one with them. It doesn't matter if we've been through reanastomosis or run-of-the-mill sleep regression, we all feel an electric jolt from the belly to the heart at the sound of our babies crying in the night. We all get nervous at the first sound of a cough, and most of us feel faint at the unexpected sight of our child's blood. The collective heart of motherhood skips a beat with every phone call from a hospital or a daycare. The cause of our sleeplessness may differ, but the bone-deep exhaustion is the same.

Most of the time I feel so alone I cannot imagine how anyone could relate to the desperation of having one daughter at home and one daughter so sick and so hospitalized. But every mother who hears my story puts herself in my shoes. I see how their hearts break for me and my daughters. Motherhood is a shared experience rooted in an intricate and profound love that gives way to deep empathy for our fellow moms. It is a love that makes us capable of overcoming obstacles that would have ended us before we had babies to fight for. A mother's love is so profound that if they let themselves imagine what it would be like to be in my position—if they let themselves feel it—they can almost experience my despair.

I am not alone. There are those who came before me. There are those who will come after. And there are many who have never and will never be where I am right now, but they empathize. It's real empathy—the kind that drives them to climb down into this hole and sit with me.

Their empathy gives me the wherewithal to do the only thing I know how to do when the race is long. I put one foot in front of the other and leave Margot's room. I put one foot in front of the other to get to the elevators and then to Vivienne's hospital room. The Real Life Arizona Robbins is ready to discharge us. We take pictures with her and The Advocate, who knows by now that she's stuck with me forever. The Petite Brunette shows up with a wheelchair and a cart for our things. She doesn't remember me and I choose not to hold it against her. The Advocate says I don't have to use the wheelchair, but I totally should. I agree, and I sit down. She hands me my daughter, and we take the elevators to the first floor.

I've taken these elevators every day for the last 135 days. I have made a lot of people very uncomfortable in here with my tears and my white-hot anger at God. I have seen dozens of NICU moms with their newly-discharged babies on their last ride down. On these elevators, I have been jubilant and I have been jealous. Right now, I'm letting myself experience the magnitude of this moment. This baby girl wearing neutral knitted overalls and a way-too-big yellow turban with a knot in the center is coming home with me. This baby girl who was not expected to live is sitting in my lap in the hospital's valet loop, in awe of the wind hitting her porcelain skin. I have spent many nights awake wondering how I would explain to people that I *was* a mother, but my daughters died. Today my Vivienne is very much alive.

I didn't tell my parents Vivienne was coming home. I didn't want to get their hopes up. An unfortunate side effect of four-and-a-half months in the NICU is that I lie in wait for shoes to drop and expectations to shatter. I also wanted to be in the room with them when they found out their first grandchild was home. A call seems insufficient for a time such as this. I ask them to come by our house to have dinner with Jerod and me. I am worried I'll blow the surprise just by virtue of leaving the hospital, so I add that I am eager to see the cactus mural Velvet Voice painted in the twins' nursery. If my father is suspicious that I'm leaving the hospital for the first time in five weeks, he doesn't let on.

The Committee of Real and Actual Car Seat Safety rolls a cart to the curb so we can buckle Vivienne into her car seat under their judging eyes. She looks impossibly tiny; it is unfathomable that she once weighed only a sixth of what she does today. I can't remember what it felt like to hold her when she was that small. While I am so glad my daughters don't weigh one pound four ounces anymore, I am sad that we haven't even left the hospital and I've already forgotten what they felt like when they were miniature. I've forgotten the sound of their first cries when the endotracheal tubes came out. Maybe my brain is protecting itself. If I remembered it all, I would surely cease to function. The valet pulls my car up. Jerod clicks the car seat into its base. I climb into the backseat and buckle myself in with no fear of my guts falling out. It's amazing what these two bodies buckled in the backseat have healed from.

I have driven the route home from the hospital more than a hundred times, but this time I am aware of every street sign and every speed bump. Every landmark tells me how close we are to a life I have not let myself imagine. We pass the lake and make a right onto our street. We pass the yard filled with mulch instead of grass on the south side. We pass our next-door-neighbor with the most manicured lawn in the history of downtown Orlando, and we pull into our driveway. A thrill runs through me, followed by sadness, anxiety, and guilt. Margot needs me and I need her. I'm not sure if I can be OK without my eyes on her sick little body. I try to talk myself off this ledge: *she is in capable hands. I deserve to celebrate this. Vivienne deserves this celebration. She needs me too.*

We set a sleeping Vivienne in one of the cribs in her nursery. For a long time, my mom kept the cribs stowed away in boxes where I wouldn't see them. She didn't want them to make me sad. I don't know when Jerod and my dad decided we didn't need to live like the babies were going to die anymore, but they've assembled both cribs. The sight of two cribs makes me queasy. Before I can let myself feel torn in half all over again, I hear my parents let themselves into the house and come down the hallway. We hit the record button on my phone that's propped up on the windowsill. We are going to want to watch this over and over.

My mom walks into the nursery. I tell her Jerod and I were discussing whether to keep the dresser centered on the wall with the mural. She catches a glimpse of Vivienne sleeping in her crib.

"Oh my gosh, that freaked me out," she says.

I laugh nervously and ask, "What?"

"That's not your baby," she says. It sounds like a question. She repeats herself and is on her knees sobbing by the time my dad enters the room. He says he knew as soon as I told them to come over.

"Was she discharged?" He asks, unable to reconcile this reality.

Jerod laughs and says, "No. We stole her."

We cry and hug over and over. Vivienne wakes up and my mom feeds her. We keep crying and hugging. Everyone says "praise the Lord" at least a few times, but then I have to go.

This is the first time Jerod, Vivienne, my parents, and I have been in the same room in nearly two months, and it's excruciating. I am struggling to hold the joy of Vivienne's homecoming with my concern about Margot's expanding belly. Where once there was barely an inch between daughters, now there is a chasm spanning 8,976 feet. I kiss this mostly healthy baby girl I just brought home after 135 days in intensive care, and I hand her to my mother. I put on my shoes. I put one foot in front of the other until I get to my car. I drive down the street; into the parking lot; into the hospital; into the elevators. I put one foot in front of the other all the way into the room where my sick baby girl sleeps with a tube down her throat once again. *How will she survive this? How will I?*

CHAPTER ELEVEN

Sugar Water Enemas and Other Things I wish I knew Nothing About

April 28, 2020 • Part Two

When I was in the fourth grade, and my brother in the second, my parents pulled us out of public school to homeschool us. They wanted more control over our education. In addition to math and science, they wanted to teach us about Jesus, and they wanted to teach us Latin and Greek root words. We had flash cards with prefixes like *contra, dis,* and *ante*. I learned to deduce a word's meaning from its parts, and even as a nine-year-old little girl, I saw the advantage this gave me over my peers. I had never heard the fancy words the pastor used in big church, like *anachronistic* or *omnipresent*, but I could take them apart and define them. In teaching me root words, my parents fueled my love of language. Etymology became my super power, and it's never been as useful as it has been in this hospital.

I don't have a medical background, but I'm often asked if I do because I nod in understanding when I hear words like *bronchopulmonary dysplasia*. I separate the words in my head. *Broncho: windpipe. Pulmon: lung. Dys: abnormal. Plasia: formation or growth.* I may not know the details or long-term implications of this diagnosis, but I get the idea: our kids have abnormally developed lungs.

Most European languages descended from a single primitive language. We don't have records of this ancient language, but linguists have used what they know to construct a language they believe closely resembles this mother tongue. The restored language is known as Proto-Indo-European (PIE). We find root words from PIE all over the English language. The word *obstruction*, for example, is the sum of *ob*, a Latin prefix meaning "in front of" and *stere*, a word-forming element from PIE that means "to spread." That is to say, something may be spread in front of, or blocking, Margot's bowel.

Margot still poops into a bag. It's a yellow liquid that hardly resembles poop. They call it output. After her partial reanastomosis, she had normal-ish output, but later her belly became very swollen. The ostomy output stopped.

I'm looking at The Possibility Doctor, hoping for an indication this is not as dire as it appears. He orders X-rays, and says he'll be back when the X-ray tech arrives; so I wait. I've been waiting for four and a half months. I've waited for hours, my thighs sticking to the reliable blue chair. I've waited in the NICU lobby. I've waited in my car, parked in the hospital's garage. One would think I would get better at this—that I would learn not to let my heart and my stomach become sick over worst-case scenarios before they happen. But I'm not waiting for a call from a mechanic about the cost of repairs. I am living in fear of irreparable news.

NOT WHAT I HAD IN MIND

I hear the familiar roll of the portable X-ray machine enter the pod. I step out of the room to avoid radiation exposure. My daughters have had innumerable X-rays. Yet, the effects of radiation are so dangerous that I shouldn't even be in the room when it happens. I pull out my phone and make a note: *how to mitigate the effects of X-ray radiation?* Modern medicine comes at a cost. An X-ray may diagnose the problem and save her life today, but what happens later? No one can tell me if we will spend the rest of my daughters' lives in hospitals combatting the aftermath of these lifesaving measures.

The Possibility Doctor excuses himself from another patient's room across the pod to join me. We step into the room and look at the screen. The images show air in her bowels where there should not be air, but it is not enough to diagnose a bowel obstruction. Before he orders more tests, he is going to consult surgery.

"You'll be here, right, mom?" he asks.

"I'll be here," I reply.

Sometimes, ignorance delays heartache or buys us time to hope. But my heart cannot take the delay of inconclusive results today. I need to know. I need a plan to resolve the problem.

Behemoth Hands arrives to dilate the ostomy. In theory, if we can create space in the bowel, the obstruction may resolve itself. I am all for a simple fix, but I know it won't work. Call it mother's intuition, but I need only to look at my lethargic daughter's swollen belly to know this is surgical. Before he starts, he expresses condolences, as if I've lost someone. Everyone knows this is a loss for me. We thought we'd be taking her home by now; instead, we may be taking her to surgery. He sticks a silicone straw through Margot's stoma, as far into her intestines as it will reach. Nothing comes out, and now she's crying around her endotracheal tube.

Behemoth Hands puts in orders to pump some kind of fluid into Margot's ostomy before getting more films. Theoretically, if there is no obstruction, this will push the air they saw in the first X-ray into her stomach. I step out of the room and the X-ray tech gets her images. I look at them, but all I can make out are puffy loops of bowel. I've seen so many X-rays of my daughters' insides, but I still don't know what I'm looking at. I have to wait until a real and actual medical doctor can translate.

Each side of the double room Margot is living in has a Murphy bed that comes down from the wall. They are a relic from an era when the babies in these rooms were not so critical and complicated, a time when doctors believed babies like mine could not survive. The beds remind the old-school nurses of simpler times when there weren't so many rules, so many lawsuits, so many tiny babies. They don't let parents use the Murphy beds anymore, but since I don't plan to leave Margot's side until this not-so-little problem is resolved, the nurse manager offers me the bed. This is not a good sign.

It's after midnight and I am sleeping on the Murphy bed when The Real Life Arizona Robbins arrives for evening rounds. It's weird they call them evening rounds, since it's the middle of the night, but I don't work here so I cannot make their semantic failures my concern. Usually, all the drama happens during morning rounds, but when I wake, acutely aware of my repugnant breath, I can tell there is news. The Real Arizona sits down next to me on the bed.

NOT WHAT I HAD IN MIND

She tells me the fluid from the fistulogram did not push the air anywhere. While this gives me a conclusive diagnosis, it is decidedly not what we were hoping for. Margot has a bowel obstruction. She will need surgery to resection the bowel.

I can't say anything. I let tears run down my face and into my lap. *How much can one person take?* I'm not sure if I say it out loud or just to myself. Regardless, The Real Arizona hears it. She takes my hands in hers. She looks into my eyes and without blinking she says, "Listen to me, we are going to get Margot home. It will not be easy. It will not be fast, but we are going to figure it out." She puts her arm around my shoulder and she says nothing else, but all the words she isn't saying hang between us.

The Real Arizona isn't a mother yet, but she will be, and when her little boy comes into the world too soon and too small, I will deliver postpartum panties, a pumping bra, and preemie clothes. I will drop off dinner. My heart will hurt for her because, even though she knows more than anyone that her 32-weeker will be OK, it's different to be a mother than it is to be a physician. Everything I do for her will feel insufficient compared to the compassion she's shown me.

Despite having the most comfortable sleeping situation Pod 1 has seen in decades, I don't sleep. I am guilt-ridden that I'm spending Vivienne's first night home away from her. I am nauseous with worry about what tomorrow holds. I am not entirely sure what a bowel obstruction means for Margot's future, but I know the more surgeries she has, the higher her risk for future bowel obstructions. I know repairing an obstruction will probably require removing part of her intestines. Surgery fixes the immediate, life-threatening problem, and it has great potential to create more problems.

I wake up to Behemoth Hands and my favorite PA discussing Margot. My breath is still repugnant and my matted mane would render me unapproachable anywhere else, but they are unfazed. They have a surgery to plan.

Since the discovery of Margot's micro colon five weeks ago, we've been administering sugar water enemas in hopes that pushing sweet water up her butt will stretch the colon and stimulate growth. I say "we" because I have been an active participant in this ungodly act every day since we started. The plan is to do these enemas until she has her full reanastomosis around the time she turns one.

Behemoth Hands (whose hands are no longer bigger than my babies) wants to do a barium enema study to check the status of Margot's colon. If he is going to open her again, he only wants to do it once. More surgeries mean more complications. He is stoic about his goal to do just one more surgery on Margot. He does not want to get my hopes up. A micro colon rarely turns into a typical colon in 45 days, but it's worth a look.

For the barium enema, a white powder is mixed with water and pushed through a small tube up Margot's rectum. Margot doesn't know anything about anything. She cannot understand this medically necessary intervention will save her life. And maybe it doesn't matter because she won't remember, but I can't help thinking that her body will remember. This child is going to need so much therapy.

The contrast solution coats the colon, making it easier to see what's going on in the images from the CT. If the nurse and the tech know what the images mean, they aren't letting on. Margot's belly has grown even more distended. It looks like an emergency to me, but the nurse and the technician go about their work. They tell me the radiologist has to read the scans, and we should know in a few hours.

When you are a child, someone telling you to wait 30 minutes after eating to get into the pool is preposterous. They may as well be telling you to wait 30 years. As we enter adulthood, we experience the speeding up of time. We realize we can't stop our hair from greying and our skin from creasing. We experience a little desperation because we can't keep our toddlers tiny. We start to think about what we want to do with our bodies and our minds before they are gone. I may look like my body and mind will soon be gone, but today I am experiencing the dragging of time like a three-year-old.

The Rockstar is a nurse practitioner with a white-blonde pixie cut that has more volume than a Led Zeppelin concert. She is super fit, wears dramatic black eyeliner, and looks like a modern Cleopatra. In my next life I want to come back as her. She is the liaison between the NICU and the pediatric surgery team. I love The Rockstar, but she only comes around pre-surgery and post-surgery, and I have come to associate her with bad news.

She starts with the bad news: we are going to surgery tomorrow, and—as usual—we won't really know what we are working with until we get in there. We don't know how much bowel has been affected by this obstruction. We don't know how much bowel she stands to lose. We don't know how much we are about to alter her quality of life. But then, The Rockstar shocks me with this: the contrast enema showed a normal-sized colon. Five weeks ago, Margot had a micro colon and she was going to go home with a poop bag until she was at least a year old. Today, The Rockstar is telling me that my second-born daughter could come back from surgery with no more assembly required.

The last 48 hours have been an exercise in holding conflicting emotions. Vivienne is home. Margot is here. A bowel is obstructed, but we found a functioning colon. No matter how many times my miracle comes through, I have not yet learned to expect miracles. The veritable miracle will be the day I stop expecting things to fall apart.

CHAPTER TWELVE

Miracles, Medicine, and Misfortune

May 2, 2020

Sixteen days after Margot was first extubated, a neonatologist I didn't know called me in the middle of the night. I had been a NICU mom for 70 days. My daughters had been to surgery half a dozen times between the two of them, and no one had ever called me from the hospital in the middle of the night. When you have two hospitalized children, no one calls you in the middle of the night with good news. She told me Margot's ostomy had become very prolapsed. It was sticking out much further than it had been earlier in the day—too far out—and it was dusky. She knew this was not the first time I'd heard this word. She didn't explain that dusky was not a word you wanted to hear when talking about an organ that should be bright red with blood flow. She told me a surgeon came by and—quite literally—pushed Margot's guts back in. We would have to wait and see if it would perfuse. I waited for her to say something like, "and now she's dead," or "it didn't go well, and we need your consent to take her to the OR," but she didn't. It didn't sound like an emergency, so I went back to sleep.

Jerod went to the hospital early in the morning because I was eager to know how Margot was doing, but I needed to pump before I left. He had not been gone 20 minutes when he called to tell me Margot coded. Time stopped, and the bedroom walls spun around me. *Please, God. No.*

He told me they had re-intubated her and she was OK, which seemed like a strange way to describe a baby who had just died and come back to life. I asked how long it took to get her back, and he didn't seem to understand what I was asking. Jerod had not spent the last ten years of his life studying a prime time medical drama. The verb *to code* was new to him. He didn't understand what happened.

I rushed to the hospital in my pajamas, boobs still full of milk. The chaos of half a dozen medical professionals with a crash cart was long over, and Margot was peacefully sleeping with the tube down her throat. The Godfather ran Margot's code. He is not on our team of tiny baby doctors, but he's now saved both my daughters' lives, and I'm quite fond of him. The Possibility Doctor said we would eventually need a head ultrasound to see if the lack of oxygen caused any brain damage. In the end, the ultrasound results were clean.

My almost-dead daughters' bodies had been in pieces, but now they were both whole. They were all but destined to die, but now they have whole lives ahead of them. And while I am very grateful to God for his mercy on my family, I am also very conflicted about God.

NOT WHAT I HAD IN MIND

My favorite couple of episodes of *Grey's Anatomy* are the ones where Jackson Avery, head of plastic surgery, attending ENT, and one of the most beautiful men on earth, wrestles with what he believes about God after experiencing a miracle. In season 15, Jackson's ex-wife, April—whom he loves and with whom he co-parents their daughter—is in a car accident. Prior to the accident, April and Jackson split up because of spiritual differences. She sees God as alive, and Jackson sees him as non-existent. The accident leaves April in a coma; they don't know if she'll ever wake up. Jackson sits by her bed, holds her hand, and starts to pray. He's never uttered a single word to God, and he says, "I want to believe. I will believe...I'll do whatever you want. I'll do anything... if you exist, just don't take her away." April squeezes his hand. He is shocked; she squeezes again and opens her eyes. This answered prayer is the catalyst for his mustard-seed-sized faith.

Sometimes, I have mustard-seed-sized faith, but right now I'm sitting in the blue chair holding Margot four days post-surgery. The surgery put her back together, but robbed her of 24 centimeters of small intestine. She is recovering slowly, but recovering nonetheless. The same cannot be said for her roommate.

As I hold Margot, I watch blood drain from a baby's body into a catheter bag. Margot's nurse has drawn the curtain around our side of the room, but I can see just enough, and I cannot look away. She is not a tiny, premature baby. She is a full-term, full fat, beautiful baby in the part of the NICU where the sickest babies come to live or die. There are a dozen medication pumps next to her warmer. The nurse is outwardly composed, but her energy is frantic. She's leaving a voicemail for the parents, telling them to get to the hospital as soon as possible. She doesn't say their baby is going to die, but that is what she means. Their baby is going to die. They must not have understood the gravity of their daughter's condition because they were out to dinner. I whisper, "Please, God," pleading for a miracle for someone else's baby.

Mirus, meaning wonderful, is the root word for the Latin *miraculum,* which is an object of wonder. I love the word wonder. I love the feeling you get when something is so unexpected, beautiful, and unexplainable that it leaves you in this state of pure admiration. The word miracle has evolved from its Latin roots. In the 12th century, the Old French word *miracle* meant a wondrous work of God. This little girl needs a wondrous work of God.

The Real Life Arizona Robbins slips through the curtain. She squats down next to the blue chair and, with very sad eyes, she tells me she hates to do this, but she needs me to put Margot back in her bed and go downstairs for a while. She helps me with the tubes and wires, and by the time Margot is back in her bed and I'm slipping through the curtain, there's a mother mourning the loss of her daughter on the other side of the room. I pinch my tongue between my teeth to stifle a sob, and I dart out of the pod, out of the NICU, into the elevators, and through the lobby. Once outside the hospital, I break into a sprint. I climb three flights of stairs and take 63 steps across the long end of the garage before arriving at my car. I open the door, get inside, and lock the door. I scream and cry. My clothes grow wet with despair, and my throat feels raw. I do not understand how God works.

NOT WHAT I HAD IN MIND

Why are my babies still here and this beautiful, full-term beauty is gone?

For the 150 days I've been in the NICU, my prayers have been unrefined: *Please, God. Why, God? Help. I'll do anything.* The answered prayers have grown my faith, but unanswered prayers make me wonder if this life is just a game of prematurity roulette. I wonder if God is really paying attention to us or are my daughters' lives a lucky statistical anomaly?

Following April's resurrection on *Grey's Anatomy*, Jackson and his new girlfriend, Maggie, are walking to work and are almost hit by a car. At the last second, their colleague, Andrew DeLuca, pulls them out of harm's way. The driver ends up hitting a young cyclist who sustains injuries that would have surely killed her if this were real life. At the end of the episode, Jackson reflects on a conversation he and Maggie had before they were almost killed, where she described faith as trusting in a giant hand that would catch you. "And then literally a hand pulled us out of the path of death," he says. Maggie tells him the hand was not God's, it was DeLuca's.

"I prayed, and April woke up," Jackson says to her.

"Or April woke up because I'm a really excellent doctor," Maggie replies.

This conversation between fictional characters epitomizes my internal dialogue about miracles. I have seen babies brought back from the dead and now I've seen this: a baby who should have lived, but didn't. I am no longer under the impression that if I believe in God—that if I pray and read the Bible—everything will work out. I know God rewarded his people for their faithfulness. I also know he let them wander around in the desert for

40 years. Shit happens, even when you believe in God. In watching this baby bleed out, I realize we don't know as much as we pretend to know about God. Sometimes we get miracles; sometimes we get medicine, and sometimes we get very sad circumstances.

I drive home sobbing. By the time I pull into the driveway, I have nothing left. I open the front door and walk to the back of my house where I find Vivienne sleeping in her crib. I scoop her up and hold her body flush with mine. I wish I could put her all the way back inside me. I am desperate to protect her from this world, desperate to protect her from any more suffering. I sit in the oversized beige rocking chair in the corner of her nursery, and I wonder what I will teach her about God. She is a miracle. Her life and her sister's life can be explained by wondrous acts of God and really excellent doctors. I know God wanted them here. I know God heard the pleas from around the world for my daughters' lives, but I don't know why he didn't hear my plea for the full-term baby girl whose parents were at dinner while she died.

I made a choice when I set foot in the hospital the night before Vivienne was born that no matter what happened, I wouldn't lose my faith. I came into the hospital believing that God is able and can bring the dead and the doomed back to life; and even when he doesn't, he is still God. Back then, I'd never seen the dead brought back to life, and I'd never heard a mother mourn. I still believe God is God. I still believe in a God who can do immeasurably more. But now, I also believe we don't have a clue how God works. The human mind wants things to make sense. We want loops that close and logical explanations, but we will never know why some babies suffer and die, or why some babies suffer and live, or why some babies never suffer at all.

When these questions overwhelm me, I try to ground myself in what I know is true. What I've seen in this hospital will continue to shape me, and God will continue to be God.

Miracles are big, wondrous acts of God; miracles are also excellent doctors, g-tubes, and broad-spectrum antibiotics. Suffering is inevitable, but it can be a catalyst for a beautiful perspective. God is big and complicated and we will never have him all figured out.

CHAPTER THIRTEEN

God Doesn't Fucking Care

June 8, 2020

Today is Margot's 174th day in neonatal intensive care. Normally, a baby of her size who has failed extubation as many times as she has would have a trach—a hole in her throat to connect a semi-permanent ventilator.

"If we need to talk about a trach, let's talk about a trach," I tell The Possibility Doctor and The Real Life Arizona Robbins during morning rounds.

"She doesn't need a trach," The Real Arizona tells me, pulling up Margot's most recent chest X-ray.

"The problem is not the lungs," The Possibility Doctor says.

"If we thought we needed to talk to you about a trach, we would be talking to you about a trach. I promise." The Real Arizona adds.

They assure me the problem is Margot's belly. It's been four weeks since the surgery that put her back together, but her belly is more swollen than it's ever been. The Possibility Doctor tells me her intestines and her enlarged organs (a side effect of the total parenteral nutrition) are pushing up on her lungs. Her lungs aren't strong enough to push back, so she can't get a good breath. In theory, the swelling will go down or the lungs will grow and this problem will be resolved. This is all fine and good, but today Margot is vomiting thick, brown sludge, and she hasn't pooped. The battle between her belly and her lungs doesn't explain this.

With as many complications as we've had, emesis has not been one of them. Neither of my kids have had so much as a spit up in their nearly six months of life. Thus, we can't exactly write this off as typical preemie reflux. The Advocate is our nurse today. I try to read her face to get an indication of how concerned I should be. Since Margot is on a ventilator, the puke comes up through a tube called a replogle. It's like a straw that goes into her upper esophageal pouch to suck out gas, saliva, and secretions. This is supposed to help with her distended abdomen, but in my unprofessional opinion it's not working. The Possibility Doctor says the emesis isn't particularly concerning since it's brown. "If it turns green, I will worry," he says.

I sit by Margot's bed, reading *Harry Potter and the Chamber of Secrets*. The Real Arizona is a big Harry Potter fan. She told me about a 23-weeker whose parents read Harry Potter to her throughout her turbulent NICU stay, and it inspired me. I am an avid reader, but I've always preferred nonfiction. I was 11-years-old and homeschooled when *Harry Potter and the Sorcerer's Stone* was published. My conservative parents did not have hard rules against witchy literature, but they didn't exactly encourage it, so I never got around to reading

Harry Potter. And since I never watch a movie without reading the book, I never saw those, either.

My love for literature has grown exponentially since childhood, and I am almost glad I waited until now to delight in the characters of this world of wizardry. I appreciate them more deeply than I would have in 1997. Margot and I are desperate to find out who (or what) is turning Hogwarts students into stone, but right before the big reveal, the replogle sucks green vomit from Margot's belly. The Advocate and I look at each other. Without exchanging a single word with me, she calls The Possibility Doctor.

He arrives. He inspects. He is quiet for a long time before he expresses concern it could be another obstruction. In the words of the great philosopher of my time, Taylor Alison Swift, "I think I've seen this film before, and I didn't like the ending."

Incompatible with life is the medical term for when a diagnosis is going to kill you. Margot lost 24 centimeters of her small intestine in the bowel resection that cleared her obstruction. Another obstruction would almost certainly mean the loss of more bowel. There comes a point when a person has so little bowel left that their condition is incompatible with life. I dart out of the room and down the hall. I exit the NICU and head straight to the bathroom. I vomit into the trash bin. *What are you doing here, God? Did you really bring us all the way here to let her die now? Does this amuse you? What kind of glory does a baby with no bowels bring you? Why? Why? Why?*

My mind revisits the thoughts about what it might be like to raise one daughter without the other. When is the right time to explain to a little girl that she had a sister who shared every bit of her DNA? How do you tell her she had a sister who shared a hospital room with her for months and months? How do you explain to a little girl that she had a sister, but now she doesn't?

Jerod leaves work to come to the hospital. We sit at Margot's bedside, and I tell him I don't understand why God would let my daughter suffer like this just to take her after six months in the hospital. I asked God to take my daughters quickly and painlessly if he wasn't going to let me raise them, so why are we here?

"God is in control," my husband tells me, and he believes it.

"Look around," I tell him. "I saw a full-term baby girl die in that bed over there."

I remind him I did everything I was supposed to do to keep my daughters safely inside, yet motherhood has been mostly suffering for me.

"God doesn't fucking care," I hiss at him.

This renders Jerod silent. Where I have questioned my faith during this season, Jerod has clung to his. The spiritual disparity between us scares him.

The Rockstar walks into the quiet tension of Margot's room. Her eyes are watery; she is almost whispering as she explains that the emesis is quite concerning. What I hear is: this is so, *so* bad. As of today, The Rockstar has seen my daughters through ten surgeries. After the obstruction, we joked about how we hoped to never see each other again within these walls. Anyone who has lived in a good hospital for months on end will tell you the staff becomes your family. The Rockstar has seen me through some of my most dire moments. She has been the bearer of bad news and she has been the deliverer of supreme relief. Her words are professional; her eyes reveal heartbreak.

Our next step is a small bowel follow-through. The Advocate pumps two ounces of barium into Margot's feeding tube. Two ounces doesn't seem like very much. A newborn baby can drink two ounces of milk every two hours—at least! Margot is older than a newborn baby, but she's never had more than five milliliters of milk in her belly at a time. This is 12 times that amount. I am sure her swollen belly will burst, but I don't have enough letters after my name to debate this. Her real and actual doctors have gotten us this far, so I have to trust they won't blow her up today. The familiar rumble of the X-ray machine comes around the corner. We get an X-ray, and then we wait. Fifteen minutes later, the rumble returns. For an hour and a half, we do this dance: image, wait, rumble, image, wait, rumble. Each 15-minute increment feels longer than the last. The Advocate doesn't read X-rays and the tech will not talk. We are in purgatory—again!

Margot doesn't throw up anymore, but I have no reason to find peace in this. Historically, her abdominal X-rays don't end well. By the time The Real Arizona arrives, I've been waiting so long, she practically has to excavate me from my tomb in the blue chair. She is smiling. I wonder if she's lost her mind. Maybe the situation is so bad she has to laugh to keep from crying. That happens to me a lot. She sits on the armrest of the blue chair like a close friend would. Her body language is not that of a person about to deliver tragic news, but when I look into the warmer that holds my tranquilized daughter, I don't see how The Real Arizona could be here to deliver anything other than disaster.

"The X-rays showed that everything moved normally through Margot's intestines," she reports.

For as long as I've been in this neonatal intensive care unit, the nurses and doctors have advised me to look at the baby. Pulse oximeters are finicky, but a baby who is blue in the face from lack of oxygen is always telling the truth. Could it not be the case that this X-ray machine is telling lies? I extend my arm with palm facing up and gesture at my daughter. My raised eyebrows tell The Real Arizona to *look at the baby*.

She wants to give it time. I want to give myself some of Margot's sedatives, but they still don't do adults here, so I trudge on. Jerod goes home to Vivienne. I make my bed in the blue chair. My Murphy bed privileges are suspended because, evidently, there's nothing life-threateningly wrong with Margot today.

I don't believe there is nothing wrong. I have been gambling with prematurity for six months. This has to be a complication or a death sentence. This has to be something—something I cannot do anything about. I sit. I watch. I wait.

It's strange to watch yourself succumb to neurosis. The pressure cooker I've been in is releasing steam in the form of obsessive behaviors. I check Margot's replogle every 20 seconds for hours. I stare at her swollen belly pondering whether it looks bigger or smaller or just the same. If she so much as stirs to indicate she is awake, I ask The Advocate if I can measure Margot's belly again. She tells me she loves me and all, but I cannot measure the belly again. She orders me to take a walk.

It is a solid 100 degrees outside, but this does not stop me from walking circles around the hospital. My mind mimics the motion, around and around. When Jerod and I were first dating, I would dizzy myself creating narratives about why I hadn't heard from him. Instead of telling me to get a freaking grip, my friend Kelli would ask me, "What are the facts?"

The facts are: the X-ray didn't show anything suspicious; Margot's belly is swollen; she threw up twice; she hasn't pooped; there is no diagnosis; I cannot fix this. I take one more walk around the hospital and sip a coffee in the cafeteria for a while before I make my way back upstairs. I scrub with scalding water, and I walk back to Margot's room pondering whether my cuticles will ever recover from our stay in the neonatal intensive care unit. The Advocate is giving a report to the nurse with the Perfect Eyeliner; when she says, "There have been no further incidents, and her belly measured smaller this afternoon."

"What?" I interrupt.

The Advocate just shrugs her shoulders and smiles before heading home for the night. I help Perfect Eyeliner change Margot's diaper, weigh her, and take her measurements. The facts are: her diaper is loaded with poop, which does not happen to people with bowel obstructions. She's lost weight, and her girth is down two-and-a-half-centimeters. Sometimes babies don't feel well and they throw up. When you're wired to expect tribulation, vomit is never just vomit. But maybe it can be? Maybe I can allow myself to be expectant—maybe I have to believe because I want them to believe. My daughters have not died; for this reason, I want them to live full of hope. I want them to believe in impossible things because they *are* impossible things.

CHAPTER FOURTEEN

Vivienne's Mom by Day; Margot's by Night

June 11, 2020

I am 34 years old today. Like any other day of my life as a NICU mother, I pull on my uniform: ultra high-waisted compression leggings and an oversized henley. It's the middle of the summer and I'm still wearing long sleeves and thick fabrics to cover myself. I have neither the energy nor the will to purchase clothes that fit this new body, a body that's not pregnant, but still carrying the effects of pregnancy.

I am sweating through my henley by the time I have Vivienne, her oxygen tank, and her pulse oximeter loaded into the car. As soon as I have secured the tank and buckled her, her belly rumbles and something erupts from under her, oozing out the leg holes of her onesie. She smiles; I weep. I unbuckle the harness and the seatbelt. I hang the oxygen tank over one shoulder and the pulse oximeter over the other before lifting the baby from her seat. I open the door to the house and yell for my mother.

Mom walks under the arch from the kitchen to the entryway. I weep some more. She laughs. We rush to the nursery on a mission. Vivienne lies on the changing table admiring the cactus mural on the wall, oblivious to the inconvenience. My mother and I undress Vivienne and disconnect her from the oxygen tank long enough to pull her soiled onesie off the tubing. We dress her and thread the tubing through the neck of the new onesie. I reconnect her to the oxygen tank and strap the tank over one shoulder and the pulse oximeter over the other. My mother holds my daughter and we walk shoulder-to-shoulder down the hallway, careful not to separate the baby too far from the tank. We remain this way through the living room, under the arch, and out the door to the car. The car seat was spared of stool, so we buckle the baby and secure her equipment. I whisper a thank you to my mother, and we're off.

Over the last seven weeks, I've mastered the dance of buckling and unbuckling while juggling medical equipment. Chauffeuring and advocating for Vivienne while still living in the NICU with Margot felt impossible at first, but somehow I've prevailed.

The first time I took Vivienne to a doctor's appointment was also the first time I had ever connected her to her portable oxygen tank. I reviewed the instructions I had jotted down on my phone and I followed them with the utmost caution for fear of depriving my eldest of oxygen. The perfect reading on her pulse oximeter indicated her transfer to the portable tank was successful, so I toted my baby and all of her equipment to the car. Before I could get her buckled into the seat, her bowels rumbled and we were back inside for a diaper and wardrobe change. We had three wardrobe changes before we ever got the kid buckled into her seat.

When I was finally settled in the driver's seat—ready for all the doting I anticipated at that first pulmonology visit—the pulse oximeter started beeping. *Your baby is not getting enough oxygen*, it wailed. I put the car in park, set myself free, and opened the back door. I checked the oxygen line and checked the settings on the tank; everything looked fine. I gave her a little boost of oxygen just in case; then I remembered the cardinal rule of parenting: look at the baby. I gazed into the car seat to find my perfectly content daughter kicking her feet. There was my culprit: a baby beating her bootie against the seat. New parents think a pulse oximeter will give them peace of mind, but the thing cannot get a read on a kid who is moving, so all it really gives us is anxiety. I got back into the front seat flustered and sweating. I put the car in reverse and promptly backed into a giant ceramic planter on my front porch.

In that moment, I hated the design of the driveway and the stupid jumbo ceramic planter we didn't even use. I hated the pulse oximeter that—in this day and age—could not differentiate between a baby kicking and a baby dying. I hated the doctors' appointments that governed our lives, and I hated that I didn't have my other baby in the back seat causing trouble with her sister.

Today, in the parking lot of the gastroenterologist's office, I exude the confidence of a seasoned mother with a medically complex child. I load the supplies into the bottom of the stroller, and I unhook the car seat from its base and click it into place. I slip the diaper bag onto my back. I loop the straps to my KN95 mask around my ears and stretch the mask across my face. The automatic doors slide open for us, and I smile. S*uccess! We have arrived.* I check in at the front desk and roll the stroller to the waiting area. Before I can even take my seat, they call us.

"Freeland, Vivianna, Vivi en eh, Viveen, Vine? Freeland," he calls, exasperated by my daughter's name.

"Vivienne," I say.

"Right, Vivienne," he acknowledges, before he measures and weighs her. He writes down his findings, and ushers us into a room where we wait for the gastroenterologist.

Growth charts, percentiles, and terms like *weight-to-height ratio* are irrelevant to most people without children. But to parents, they are the beginning of a lifetime of comparing our children to their peers. From the moment we bring a baby into our family and roll them into their first doctor's appointment, we're given numbers and charts. Some of us get praise and some of us get questions like, "How often is she eating?" or "How many ounces is she taking?" Those of us on the receiving end of such questions feel insecure, as though we—despite all our efforts—are at fault for this child who is small for her age. But should it feel that way? There is, after all, a first percentile because one percent of children fall into it. When your baby is in the first percentile, it makes them seem like a tiny rarity, but one percent of the 3.7 million babies born each year is 37,000. My tiny baby is not alone.

I'm holding a six-month-old who should be a two-month-old, so I get double the numbers and double the charts. The gastroenterologist comes into the room with two stacks of papers: one for her actual age, and another for her age adjusted for how old she would be if I had carried her to term. He is an especially tall, lean man with skin the color of dark wheat. His hair is black with a light peppering of gray. He greets me and my daughter, and he warms up the stethoscope with his hand before pressing it to her belly.

"How often is she eating?"

"Every two-and-a-half to three hours, even at night."

"How many ounces is she taking?"

"Two ounces, sometimes a little more."

"Hmmm. Any diarrhea or vomiting?"

"No."

Vivienne does not even fall into the first percentile for her actual age. When we adjust for prematurity and compare her to two-month-olds instead of six-month-olds, she is still tiny, the 20th percentile, but it doesn't seem like cause for concern. At least I don't think so, and I'm practically a doctor now.

The gastroenterologist directs my attention to her growth chart. He points out that she's tiny. I wonder if (since we're pointing out the obvious) I should inform him he is very tall. He draws a line with his fingers between the dot of her last weigh-in and the dot of today's weigh-in; then he flips the page and traces the line between her last and current length measurements.

"She's gaining weight well, but her length hasn't changed," he tells me. "We have to watch that. She may need growth hormones if she doesn't start growing taller."

I nod in acknowledgment, but a wave of fury washes over me. *Why would he even mention this? How much could he possibly expect my daughter to grow in two weeks? A centimeter? Half a centimeter?* I want to ask him to measure her again. Maybe the medical assistant made a mistake.

To measure a baby who can't stand, the medical assistant lays the child down on a piece of paper and marks a line atop the baby's head. While holding the baby in place, so her head stays glued to the first line, he stretches her leg and makes another mark at the heel of her foot. For an infant, a centimeter is the difference between growing and not growing enough. That is to say, the difference between growing and not growing enough could be a medical assistant who was a little off with his pen. *Would this be a good time to demand a recount?*

I came here wanting praise because this kid who was not expected to live is rolling up to the gastroenterologists' office heavier than she was last week; instead I got something new to worry about. I did not need something new to worry about.

I am holding two fragile lives in my heart and the tension is stretching me thin. Vivienne's mother is ruled by trying to fit quality time into a calendar full of doctors' appointments, while Margot's mother lives in the walls of the hospital hoping for good news, but preparing for disaster. If I crumble and I weep every time my expectations splinter, I will waste the energy I should be using to love my daughters—to breathe their scents and relish their expressions. I don't feel pressure to be strong. I just don't have time to waste on weakness.

I leave the gastroenterologist's office with my head held high because I'm choosing not to worry about a centimeter today. The numbers on his chart must have distracted this doctor from looking at the baby—the rosy-cheeked, pudgy-thighed beauty with a stork's bite between her eyebrows. My daughter doesn't need growth hormones. She needs time and maybe someone who is more accurate with a ballpoint pen. I unclip the car seat from the double stroller and click Vivienne's seat into its base. I look at the attachment intended for a second car seat, and I laugh at the idea of rolling into this office with two tiny babies tangled in tubing. I collapse the stroller and decide we will see a different gastroenterologist when Margot comes home—one with optimism and a sense of humor who doesn't worry me before it's time.

I drive my firstborn home and place her in her *abuela's* arms. I take a two-minute shower and smear some moisturizer on my face. I stare at myself in the mirror. The woman I see resembles someone I used to know, but she's different. Some might say the exhaustion she wears under her eyes has aged her. They are not wrong. She is older, but she is also stronger and more resilient than she was just six months ago.

I refill my hospital bag with clean pump parts, snacks, and a book about gut health—everything I need to transition into my role as Margot's mother. I kiss Vivienne goodbye and travel the well-worn road back to the hospital.

I am 34 years old today. A year ago, a life like this was unfathomable. If I had heard a story like mine, I would have responded with something like, "I could never survive that. I would die." But today, for the sake of my daughters, I remain standing. It is heartbreaking and it is beautiful. It is agony and it is awe.

CHAPTER FIFTEEN

The Longest Way Home

June 2020

Margot is six months old and she's pissed. She still has a breathing tube down her throat, and she is more aware of it than she has ever been. Her agitation is so fierce that the neonatalogists started her on a Precedex drip, a sedative also used to treat acute agitation in schizophrenia patients. Despite the tranquilizers, she doesn't sleep, and I can't blame her. I can't sleep here either. Pod 1 is raucous. The sickest babies on the unit are all here with their alarms ringing and their nurses swarming. One-pound babies are born at all hours of the night and they are rushed up here with hordes of nurses, respiratory therapists, and physicians giving orders in their outside voices.

I didn't notice the noise when it was my kids causing chaos, but now that Margot can't rest, I hear *everything*. Her roommates' medication pump is done, so it's beeping. In the room next door, two babies' oxygen saturations have dropped; they are beeping. In the room that shares a wall with Margot's bed, a team is rounding. The noises blend into the kind of discord that even this sedated baby and her bone-tired mother cannot sleep through.

A couple of weeks ago, The Possibility Doctor mentioned moving Margot to Pod 4. He also mentioned that, if we did that, we would have to transition Margot to a different team of doctors. That was a conversation ender for me. I don't want new doctors. I don't want a new room and new nurses. The Actual MD, The Real Life Arizona Robbins, and The Possibility Doctor have gotten us this far. They know everything about Margot. How can I let someone who hardly knows her take over?

Moving to Pod 4 doesn't just scare me because we would have new doctors. It scares me because it feels like a declaration of our intention to stay in the NICU forever. Pod 4 is the complex care unit. It's where babies go when they aren't getting better. NICU moms talk. I know the babies over there have tracheostomies and g-tubes. I know many of them are approaching their first birthdays, while for some it's already come and gone. When I imagined two separate celebrations for Margot and Vivienne's birthdays, I did not imagine one would be in Pod 4.

I've been sleeping in the blue chair more often than not because Margot is so irritable at night. She needs me to comfort her. I recline the chair and pull a fluffy gray and white blanket over myself. My brother-in-law and his girlfriend gifted me this blanket when I was recovering from the C-section. When walking into someone's suffering, you can't go wrong if you bring a good blanket. This one has lived some life with me. I close my eyes and Margot's oxygen alarm starts to wail. She's fine. She's always fine. The monitor wails when it can't get a read on a restless baby, and she is always restless. I bend over the warmer and put my cheek next to hers. I cup her opposite cheek, my palm resting on the miniature pacifier in her mouth; my fingers cover her ear to block out the sound. She uses a miniature pacifier because the breathing tube does not leave room for a standard newborn paci. She stills, but I know if I move, she will be sleepless again. I keep my right hand on her cheek and I reach behind me with my left hand to grab the underside of the blue chair to roll it closer to the warmer.

The heater over Margot's bed is turned off. She is old enough and big enough to regulate her body temperature. The only reason she's still in a warmer is because it sits higher than a regular crib, allowing her tubing to safely connect to the ventilator. I rest my left forearm across the plastic siding of the warmer crib and lay my forehead on it. I close my eyes. For a long while I can't sleep because I am so frustrated at the beeping and the nurses and respiratory therapists bustling about, pushing buttons on medication pumps. *Why does everything beep here? Put that thing on silent. Get my kid some ear plugs. And please shut up.* Despite my upright position, forearm pillow, and the cacophony, I eventually fall asleep because my soul is tired.

The sun peeks through the partially opened curtain much too early. Jerod comes to relieve me. I go home. I shower. I cuddle and feed Vivienne, and I wonder how much longer I can live like this. I wonder if the heartache of a sick child—of a family separated—can wear a mother down so much that she can't get up again. Then I think of my mother raising Vivienne. She is 60 years old and she is waking up every two hours, every night, with an infant. She is exhausted. The heartache of her sick grandchildren has worn her down, but she keeps getting up again. Mothers are like this, standing through sleepless nights and hospital stays, waiting for a break in the chaos before we give ourselves permission to fall.

Jerod and I just started alternating nights at home with Vivienne and nights in the hospital with Margot. Tonight is his night. I wake up just before midnight to my phone ringing, and I panic. It's Jerod. As rehearsed, he starts the conversation by informing me nothing happened; Margot is OK. The on-call neonatologist is making her Middle of the Night Rounds. Jerod explains that she asked him what Margot is doing here. The question jars me. *Where else should we be? It's not like they're going to let me out of here with a kid on a ventilator with a gaping, infected abdominal wound.* Jerod explains that the doctor says it's too noisy in here for Margot. She'll never be able to rest. She needs to go to Pod 4. Jerod isn't asking me if I will reconsider Pod 4. He's telling me this doctor is making some calls and moving us out.

I am tired of my kid being pumped full of sedatives. I am tired of sleeping in an upright position. I am tired of bad news, and dying babies, and people asking me when I think Margot might come home. I don't fight back on this doctor's eviction notice, not because I am too tired to fight, but because I'm so tired I know something has to change.

The sun rises and shines upon the dark, puffy circles under my eyes. I kiss Vivienne goodbye, and I tell her I am so sorry her *mamá* has to go. I tell her I am so happy her *abuela* will be here to take such good care of her. I relieve Jerod at the hospital, taking my place on the blue chair. I wonder if I have sat in this chair more times than any NICU mom before me. It feels like it.

The Possibility Doctor and The Real Life Arizona Robbins are rounding this morning. My daughter is stable, and my daughter is moving to Pod 4. They insist this is a step toward home. I nod, even though it feels like the longest way home. The Advocate calls for a cart. I fold my blankets and Margot's blankets. I pack the small library of books and journals from the windowsill into an extra large diaper bag that has yet to carry any diapers.

Because Margot is still on a ventilator, it takes a team to roll her halfway around the circular pod and down the hall. On the walls hang miracles from decades past, photos of all the babies born too soon or too sick whose families are forever grateful for this place. At the end of the hallway, we make a left. We walk a little farther and into a circular pod with a nurses' station in the center and double rooms around the perimeter. It is so quiet here it feels like the Ritz-Carlton spa, not the NICU. I feel immediate relief. Rest is imminent.

The rooms here are made for two babies, just like in Pod 1, but as long as they have the space, they only keep one baby in each room. On the right side of Margot's double room is a sleeper couch where there would normally be a second baby. I feel right at home until the moment The Advocate comes to say goodbye. The nurses who have raised my daughters are tiny baby nurses. They trained to care for the smallest, most acute babies born at this hospital. They are needed in Pod 1. The nurses in Pod 4 are trained in developmentally-appropriate care for big babies who have been in the hospital a long time. The Advocate is still our primary nurse. She promises she will take care of Margot whenever she can, but we both know it will be less often than either of us would like.

She leaves and the Pod 4 nurse comes to introduce herself. She is bubbly and delighted to meet Margot. The

Freeland twins are already legends in this NICU. She has decorated Margot's walls with welcome signs and put a basket of toys under her warmer. We are not in Tiny Baby Land anymore.

A slender brunette with a bohemian kind of beauty walks in. I know her because she was the doctor on call the night Vivienne was septic, and I did my research. She is one of the two doctors who oversees the complex care unit. She is my age, Ivy League educated with a master's and a medical degree. She is kind. She is articulate. She is grounded. She is My Role Model.

She explains she is going to set up a meeting with all of Margot's specialists to discuss our next steps. The plan is to wean Margot's ventilator settings if our girl asks for it, but we're not going to push her. I am conflicted about this. All we've done for the last six months is push her to get off the ventilator. If we are giving up on that, it means we've not just changed pods; we've changed plans. The idea of letting my kid rest until she is ready is a relief. We may be here for the rest of our lives, but at least we aren't being pressured to leave.

My Role Model doesn't tell me the meeting is going to be about a tracheostomy, but I know that's what it's about. I know they want to discuss cutting a hole in my daughter's throat so she can come home on a ventilator. I have spent hours scouring the internet for stories about babies like mine. I know how this will go. In a private room with half a dozen doctors, we will talk about the risks and the months and months of recovery that have to happen before she can be discharged. I am so ready to go home I don't care what it takes to get us there. The job of parenting two little girls with very different abilities is one for which I am unqualified, but I will figure it out. I will make anything work if it means we can get out of this hospital and all be together.

Margot is resting comfortably for what feels like the first time in her life, so I tell the Pod 4 nurse I am going to run home and get sheets and blankets. She tells me I don't have to stay. *Right,* I think, *I just met you, and you think I'm going to leave my daughter in your care overnight? Definitely not, sis.* I smile and tell her it's OK, I always stay. I can tell she thinks I'm overbearing and a little insane. She is absolutely right.

I drive home in silence. The idea of this meeting sits like a gulp of too-hot coffee in the spot where my chest meets my abdomen. The coffee cools as I pull into my driveway and anticipate smushing my adorable baby. Vivienne has almost doubled in weight since she came home. She doesn't need supplemental oxygen anymore, not even at night. She holds her head high during tummy time, and when my mom sings to her, she squawks along. Seeing her thrive like this while her sister is awaiting a hole in the throat wrecks me, but seeing her thrive like this is also healing.

I have not grown accustomed to the misery of raising my twin daughters separately, of splitting my time and feeling like there's never enough of me. If anything, it's worse than it's ever been. When the girls were both in the hospital, I accepted the hospital as my home. But now, my split heart longs for reunification. What scares me the most about the tracheostomy is not the surgery or managing the medical device, it's the recovery. It's the many more months of separation. My resilience has surprised me time and time again, but it can't go on like this forever. The time is coming that even the responsibility of motherhood won't be enough motivation to get me up again. For now, though, I pack fresh sheets and blankets and I get up and go where I'm needed.

It's after dark when I arrive back at Pod 4. There are no machines beeping and the nurses are seated quietly around the station charting. The serenity of this space stands in stark contrast to the part of the hospital I've lived in for the last six months. I walk into Margot's room, and she's asleep. I seize the moment to make my bed and change into pajamas in the bathroom down the hall. By the time I return, she's awake and complaining. She flails her arms, arches her back, and kicks. I cover her ear with my palm and hold the pacifier in her mouth with my fingers; she drifts back to sleep.

The sleeper sofa beckons me. I slip under the blanket just long enough to fall asleep, but before my mind can wander too far into dreamland, Margot is complaining again. I look at the clock. It feels like I fell asleep mere minutes ago, but a whole hour has gone by since I laid in the bed. She settles and I sleep for another hour and a half, but then she's up again, crying and flailing. I check her diaper and find it soaked through. I change it, wash my hands, and put my palm against her ear, but she keeps wiggling. She can't sleep, and it doesn't surprise me. I wouldn't be able to sleep through the night either if all I'd ever known was interrupted rest. An hour goes by before Margot settles, and we both drift off to sleep until daylight comes streaming through the windows. When I wake up, I feel like a different woman—no longer on the verge of collapse. Margot looks like a different baby, a rested baby.

CHAPTER SIXTEEN

Take the Miracle and Run

July 7, 2020

Today is family meeting day.

We've been in Pod 4 for 20 days. They have been some of the sweetest and strangest 20 days of my NICU mom career. The doctors, nurses, and respiratory therapists have been committed to following Margot's lead. When we tried to wean her sedatives, she showed all the symptoms of withdrawal. Like a baby born with opioids in her system, she was sweaty, blotchy, tachyaepnic, and impossible to soothe. I held her for hours upon hours, naïvely believing I could fix this. The Pod 4 team stopped weaning the sedatives. They made a plan to slowly substitute one sedative with another that will be easier to wean when she's ready. Since they aren't going to let me take a sedated baby home, this glacial-paced wean feels like a loss. There have, however, been far more wins than losses.

In the quiet, no-pressure ambiance of the complex care unit, Margot has weaned herself off the ventilator. She has all but begged for less respiratory support, and they have made her wait before giving her what she wanted. For the first time in her life, she is off the ventilator, and she's not struggling. She is often agitated with the mask she's wearing for respiratory support. She rips it off her face, as if to say, "Look mamá, I can do it myself."

CPAP stands for continuous positive airway pressure. It's a form of noninvasive respiratory support that uses mild pressure to keep the airway open. Bubble CPAP is a form of continuous positive airway pressure for babies. It helps prevent the air sacs in a baby's lungs, called alveoli, from deflating. Margot has been on bubble CPAP once before; it wasn't enough. Her alveoli deflated. She deteriorated quickly and ended up back on a vent. It feels different this time. She is looking around the room and squawking at me to pay attention to her. Her little voice is raspy, a reminder of the countless extubations she has failed. Normally, there's a limit on how many extubations a baby can fail before they have to get a trach, but The Possibility Doctor was so sure she didn't need one. My Role Model is less sure—or maybe she *was* less sure?

Margot has made great progress, but you can't take a kid home on bubble CPAP. You can't even take a kid home on the next step down from bubble CPAP: high flow oxygen. I don't know what to expect at this meeting today. I am eager to prepare myself for whatever battle I'm fighting next. From the outside it may look like I'm just a sad mom quietly driving back and forth between the hospital and my house, alternating which of my babies I'm holding, but on the inside I'm fighting to figure out how I am going to work with what we've been dealt to give my daughters the best quality of life. I'm learning to be a physical and occupational therapist. I'm researching what to feed them to support their compromised immune systems and digestive health.

Now that Margot is breathing, I can breathe too. There is space in my head to think about something other than survival. I can picture a future, and it's not at all the future I imagined when Jerod and I decided to have children. I thought my daughters would wear the cutest clothes to *el daycare de abuela* and I would go back to work. I wanted to finish graduate school and pursue a career change. I wanted more meaningful work, a more meaningful life.

This is motherhood. I am new here, but I understand the assignment is unconditional love and the relentless pursuit of a good and meaningful life for our children. The challenge is disentangling the definition of "a good and meaningful life" from the highlight reel that is social media. I don't know if my daughters' premature brains will ever thrive in an academic environment. I don't know if their vision will be good enough for them to drive or even play team sports. Margot may need feeding therapy for years before she can eat apple slices cut into star shapes with a cookie cutter. It's unclear whether my daughters will fit into any of the boxes society deems as good and meaningful, but most moms aren't looking to stuff their babies into boxes. We are looking to shatter ceilings and defy statistics. We are looking to facilitate big, beautiful lives for our children, whatever their abilities are. And sometimes we have to lay down one version of a meaningful life and pick up a very different one.

Our priorities and our stories shape who we believe our children will be. Some of us concern ourselves with education, some worry about the state of American nutrition; others choose to concern themselves only with keeping small humans alive. We sacrifice sleep and stretch our finances to give our kids what we believe is best. We try to protect them from the things that hurt us when we were young. We suit them up with the armor we think they will need to face this broken world without it breaking them.

Margot's reanastamosis was a success, but her stool is just as loose as it was when she was only using half her intestines. She has nothing but watery, yellow diarrhea in her diaper and the more we wean the total parenteral nutrition (TPN) administered through her PICC line, the more she struggles to gain weight. She could come home on TPN, but it would complicate things, and no one wants to go that route. She would have to go back to surgery for a central venous catheter. Any kind of central line puts her at high risk for infection, though. The TPN is a catch-22 because, while it helps with growth, it's abusing her organs. She is jaundiced and her spleen is enlarged. We need to get her off the TPN. However, without it, her growth could suffer. As we've started weaning, there are days she doesn't gain any weight; other days, she loses. Add this to the list of reasons she is seven months old and still living in the NICU.

I have been reading everything I can find about short gut syndrome and rehabilitating the gut. The only thing I can do with a baby who is not ready for solids is to keep producing breast milk. I learn my milk has the potential to seed and feed Margot's gut microbiome. For a child who has been fed a steady diet of antibiotics for weeks at a time, the good bacteria from my milk is Margot's best chance at building an immune system, regulating her digestion, and reducing her risk of allergies and asthma. But my girl has been through a lot. I would be naïve to think boobie milk is enough to nurse her back to health.

It's two o'clock. Family meeting time. I am watching the entrance to Margot's double room, which I guess is also my room, since I have slept here every night for the last 20 nights. Jerod is standing next to me. Anxious is an insufficient descriptor for what I feel. There is a part of me that believes we may be together at home soon. The other part of me believes we have one baby home when both should have died, so I should just be grateful for what I have. I should not hope so big. I should not expect any more miracles.

Our nurse directs us down the hall and into a small conference room. The gang is all here: pulmonology, gastroenterology, neonatology, cardiology, and palliative care. The last of which elicits a raised eyebrow from me—*seriously, what are you doing here?* It feels strange to have so many people in the room, given the raging pandemic outside, but this is an essential meeting of essential workers.

Historically, I've known what to expect when I join a conversation about Margot's care and course of treatment. For almost seven months, these conversations have been deflating. While Margot has been steadily improving, she cannot come home with all the medications and all the respiratory support she's still requiring, and there's no guarantee we'll be able to keep weaning her. We could hit a plateau. Maybe it's because everyone is wearing masks, but I can't read the room. I cannot tell if people are here to talk about a plateau or to plan a celebration. I close my eyes and summon my inner poker player. I can always count on her to swallow her disappointment, if needed.

My Role Model welcomes everyone. "Three weeks ago, I thought we would need this meeting to plan for Margot's tracheostomy, but today we are here to plan Margot's discharge."

I gasp, and for 15 minutes a stream of tears drips down my face, rendering my mask ineffective. The plan is simple: If we keep weaning Margot's respiratory support, sedatives, and TPN at the agonizing rate we've been weaning it, she can be discharged in three weeks.

I hug everyone in that room—even the palliative care doctors, who were not in the room to talk about hospice care, but rather, to talk about weaning one of Margot's medications. (Turns out, I didn't really know what palliative care was.) Jerod and I walk down the hall and I make him vow to tell no one what was said in that room today. I am not superstitious, but I have seen how much can go wrong here in just three hours. I'm not about to let myself or anyone else get excited about what we hope will happen in three weeks.

Back in our room, I lift my daughter out of her crib. Since the ventilator is gone, she's in a crib like a regular baby. I sit in my old friend, the blue chair, and I stare at her for a good, long time. I take in the scuba mask that's pumping her full of bubble CPAP and the PICC line in her arm, pushing TPN and sedation into her veins. I take in the g-tube, and I decide that instead of hating the feeding tube for everything it is taking from us, I am going to love it for everything it's giving us. I decide if I am going to be a gastro mom, I'm going to be the very best of my kind. I will administer Margot's medications.

I will set up Margot's tube feeds. I will clean the g-tube and check to make sure it's not loose or leaking saline. By the time I take her home, I will be unintimidated by my daughter's medical complexity.

Jerod heads home to Vivienne, and I jot a prayer down in my journal. *Thank you for the miracles. Thank you for the ways you have protected and provided for Margot. Please keep us on this smooth path. Please bring our baby home to us this month.* I underline the last two words to emphasize to God that I'm trusting him enough to pray specific prayers. It's much more hopeful than the laments that fill the previous pages.

Lament comes from the latin *lamentationem*. It means to wail or weep. There's an entire book in the Old Testament called Lamentations. It's a reflection on the catastrophic fall of Jerusalem from the perspective of a survivor. It's a record of the pain that followed the destruction. Lamentations is too depressing for me right now. Instead, since we've been in the NICU, I've been reading the Psalms. Here, David, a shepherd turned King, cries out to God. I'm paraphrasing a bit, but he essentially says, "The crappier things get, the further away you are—like you don't even care." *This guy gets it.* Suffering has unearthed a lot of questions about God's character. The practice of rewriting David's laments has validated my questions, but it hasn't gotten me as many answers as I would like. Maybe I don't need answers. Maybe it's time to take my miracles and run.

CHAPTER SEVENTEEN

The Comeback Kid

July 28, 2020

For the last 48 hours, Margot's room has been a flurry of people. The Possibility Doctor, The Real Life Arizona Robbins, The Rockstar, a physical therapist, and even the pharmacist stopped by to say congratulations. We take selfies. We laugh. We cry. We shake our heads in disbelief.

"What a comeback," I say to no one in particular. "What. A. Comeback."

While discharge is one of the happiest parts of a doctor's day, it's also the least urgent. We will be waiting to leave this place all day because there are deliveries, X-rays, and intubations ahead of us. The Advocate is our nurse today, and I cannot imagine anyone else sending us off. Over the last 21 days, she and the Pod 4 nurses have been so patient as I've squirted medication into my face and all over my hands when I forget to unclamp the g-tube line. They've listened to me obsess over Margot's ever-so-slowly improving diarrhea. They've let me weigh her a dozen times every night to make sure we get the very highest weight. They have been the team that has carried us to the finish line, and now it's right there, just a few steps away.

A stout woman I've never seen before comes into the room. She introduces herself as the interim dietitian. Our regular dietitian is out today. She asks how we're doing, and I tell her today is our very best day. I tell her today we are going home. She flips through some papers in her hands for an unusually long time. She turns to The Advocate and says, "Yeah, no. This baby is not going home today." She says it like I—the mother of this child who has been waiting 224 days to take her home—is not standing right there. My mouth falls open; devastation sits in the pit of my belly. I look back and forth between my beloved nurse and this witch. She explains the obvious: Margot is on 24/7 g-tube feeds and her weight gain is subpar.

Here is the heartbreak I expected. This is why I didn't get my hopes up until today. This is why I didn't tell anyone our plan to get Margot home. I have learned to expect the worst, but this is vile. I am so paralyzed I can't even close my mouth before The Advocate looks the dietitian in the eye and tells her, "This mom has spent the better half of a year at her daughters' bedsides. She's spent the last five weeks living on this unit, changing every diaper and administering all her daughter's medications, even in the middle of the night. She knows what to do and she knows her kid better than any nurse or interim dietitian here. This baby is going home today. Thank you."

All that wicked dietitian says is, "OK," and she leaves. The anguish of hearing my daughter wasn't coming home robbed me of reason. If I had thought about it, I would have concluded that a dietitian who has never been on my daughter's case could not sabotage her homecoming once her entire medical team had decided it was time. I thank The Advocate. I pick up my daughter and I sit in the blue chair one last time. *Farewell, old friend.*

The Actual MD is on discharge duty today. He is at the nurse's station putting the finishing touches on our ticket out of here. I ask Jerod and The Advocate to help me roll Margot's oxygen tank over to him to take some photos. He hands me a discharge summary. I hand him my baby. After a couple of photos, The Petite Brunette arrives with a cart and a wheelchair. She does a double take. I assure her this is not merely the feeling of déjà vu; she has, in fact, seen this before.

We take a victory tour on our way out of the NICU to say goodbye. Jerod wants to take pictures at the discharge wall. He asks if we should send someone to find out who is in Pod 1 to get a few more pictures before we leave. I tell him we need to go before someone changes their mind and readmits my child. He thinks I am joking, but I am not.

"No more," I snap.

My therapist says expecting disaster is a normal response to trauma. It's nice of her to normalize my extreme pessimism, but I want to fix it. I see what I'm doing here. I see how I cannot allow myself to feel the significance of Discharge Day because I am panicked something will go wrong. I'm worried that nasty dietitian is lurking around the corner with a well-prepared case about why I am unfit to care for such a complicated child. *What if she's right? What if I can't do this? What if we end up back here tonight?* The celebratory gasps and spontaneous clapping from nurses and respiratory therapists in the hallways snaps me out of my downward spiral. *This is really happening. We are really going home.*

I am in a wheelchair in an elevator on my way down to the first floor of the hospital. I am holding this precious, almost-nine-pound baby girl. She's wearing a yellow floral onesie with ruffles that make it look like a dress. Her head is wrapped in a teal turban with a knot in front, just like the one her sister wore the day she was discharged. To say this is surreal would be an understatement. This is so far from where I expected we would be at the end of July that I feel like I'm watching it happen to someone else.

The Committee of Real and Actual Car Seat Safety and the valets play a mean game of Tetris as they try to fit the oxygen tanks, the pole for the feeding bag, and 224 days of stuff into the trunk of my car. We probably should have brought The Monster Truck. I am so desperate to leave that I forget to take photos of Margot strapped into her car seat. The floor of the front passenger's seat and most of the backseat are packed with medical supplies, so I climb into the front seat and over the center console to sit in the middle seat next to my gargantuan seven-month-old daughter.

We wave goodbye and drive away. It's not until we've pulled out of the valet loop that I stop holding my breath. It's not until we've pulled into our neighborhood that I believe we're going home. We are in the driveway when joy and relief wash over me. Two hundred and twenty-four days ago, I tried not to love her and her sister because I was so sure they would die, and now I'm standing on the front porch of my house with my daughter in her car seat and her sister on the other side of this door. My family—a family I didn't think I would get to raise—is going to be whole in just a second.

Jerod rings the doorbell. We obviously have a key to our house, so I'm sure this gives us away. My dad opens the door holding Vivienne. He is wearing every emotion I'm feeling on his face.

"I knew it," he bellows. "I was just pointing out the window, telling Vivi that any minute now her sister was coming home."

He may have thought he knew it, but the look on his face tells me he cannot believe it. My mom, who was in the restroom, comes around the corner and sees me holding a baby; she turns and looks at my father who is also holding a baby. It takes her a moment to process these two babies in the same room, and when she does, she falls to her knees. The moment is pregnant with gratitude and disbelief, with comfort and triumph. The happiness is overwhelming, as are all the other feelings I've suppressed for the last seven and half months. I sit on the floor at the entrance to my house and I hold my daughters together for the first time in four months. For the first time in their tumultuous little lives, I let myself think about them growing up together under this roof.

Margot's pre-discharge MRI was remarkably normal for a baby who has endured what she has. The right side of her cerebellum is marginally smaller than the left, but My Role Model told me she should develop normally. The results of this MRI likely mean that here—on the very floor where I sit—my daughters will learn to crawl, and walk, and talk. Under this roof, they will learn to love Cuban black beans and vegetable curries. They will pull ornaments off Christmas trees and throw sippy cups across the floor. Within these walls, they will make messes and maybe even learn to clean them up. It was just a house, but now it's a wellspring of memories and milestones.

The evening is a blur of spilled milk and joyful tears. I put on an air of confidence as I fill feeding bags and syringes. Per doctor's orders, Margot takes the bulk of her nutrition via her g-tube, but I can give her medication by mouth, if she wants it. And she wants it. Margot takes an antidiarrheal and an anticonvulsant to calm postoperative nerve pain. She loves the syrupy liquids, smacking her lips and sticking out her tongue for more. It is mind-boggling that instead of the oral aversion we expected, this child has an affinity for whatever flavors she can get. Her little life is full of possibility beyond anything I could have imagined for her just a month ago.

My parents haven't said anything about the tubes and the syringes, but I know it's scary and a little sad. I have to normalize it, not for them, but for my daughter. Whether we have these tubes for many years or mere months, she cannot get the impression that this is too much—that she is too much. I learned to prime feeding pumps and clamp lines during some of the hardest days of my life. They can learn, too. These buttons and beeps are a path forward. For someone who doesn't understand all the ways our story could have gone, the tangles of tubing may seem like a disappointment. But if the cost of our baby's life is a bag of milk pumped into her belly, we are getting a pretty good deal.

We alternate holding babies until they fall asleep. Vivienne has been sleeping in the nursery for months now to facilitate early morning shift changes. My mom takes her in the middle of the night and my dad in the early morning. But no one other than me is ready to take Margot. No one knows the breast milk to formula ratio or how to prime the pump. They haven't mastered the g-tube or memorized medication doses. Tonight, and for many nights to come, it's all me, just like I have prayed for it to be.

I set a sleeping Margot in the bassinet next to my bed. I use a tiny, green silicone funnel to refill the pouch of milk hanging from the IV pole with a mixture of breast milk and formula powder. I select 15ml/hr for four hours, and I start the pump. I crawl around the bassinet and onto my bed. I smush my face against the mesh so I can hear her breathe, and I fall asleep for 90 glorious minutes before Margot complains, as if to remind me she's home and she's very much alive.

I am disoriented when I open my eyes to find myself in my bed, in my home, with my daughter's bassinet within reach. For a moment, I wonder if I'm actually awake. The realization of my reality is like a bolus of caffeine. I sit up wide-eyed to look at her. She looks like a little doll. While Vivienne has fiery eyes, Margot's are wide with wonder, even when she's grumbling.

I reach my hand over the side of the bassinet and rest my palm over Margot's ear, using my fingers to hold her pacifier in place. This routine never fails. She falls asleep; then I do, and we move through a surreal cycle of sleeping and waking and refilling the feeding pump in our own home all night long.

Sleep is a luxury new parents can rarely afford, but maybe not sleeping is the real reward. Waking up in the middle of the night because your baby has enough breath in her body to cry is marvelous, but sleep deprived parents usually fail to appreciate it. I know I will grow tired of the waking and feeding and grunting one day soon, but I hope I always remember what it feels like to have my daughter waking up at home tonight. I will strive to revel in this messy middle.

PART 3: THE DIARRHEA DIARIES

CHAPTER EIGHTEEN

Imodium Lips

When you give a kid a piece of bread or a square of chocolate, they will ask for more before they are even finished. We may laugh and tell them to savor what's in front of them, as though this is some kind of hard-earned wisdom we've won. But our hearts are not any different from a greedy toddler's. When we get the job, or the house, or the miracles, we may enjoy them for a moment or a month, but we always move on to the next desire. To be human is to want more.

August 2020

Margot has been home a week, and she has barely stopped crying. She wails all day, unless I'm holding her. Sometimes, she lets other people hold her, but mostly it's me. This is unfortunate, seeing as how every feeling I resisted during our NICU stay has taken up residence in my soul, rendering me almost nonfunctional. My therapist diagnoses me with postpartum post-traumatic stress disorder and postpartum anxiety. My OB suspects postpartum depression as well. Who cares what it's called? I'm living with my brain on fire, while my body feels held down with the weight of a thousand ounces of breast milk, and I'm coping with coffee, which I'm sure is contraindicated.

Part of me wonders if Margot was not ready to live unsedated. The world is too stimulating. There are so many people in this house—grandparents, parents, and a big sister—always making noise. And all the familiar noises of the NICU are gone. Being fully alive makes you fully aware of how chaotic the world is; maybe this is why my daughter is so pissed.

I'm not convinced overstimulation is Margot's only problem. I have a longstanding theory that my kid is hungry. She's not hungry in the way one might be if they have not eaten enough. We feed her through the g-tube. We know she's getting enough nutrition. I suspect she is hungry for the pleasure and satisfaction of taste.

I've suspected this since our days in Pod 1, but until we got to the complex care unit, we couldn't do anything about it. For most of her NICU stay, Margot's respiratory support was too high for her to eat by mouth. The air being forced into her lungs made it impossible to swallow milk, but she wanted to. She gnawed on cotton swabs dipped in breast milk like they were a delicacy.

In the name of developmentally appropriate care, Margot was discharged with permission to breastfeed for two or three minutes every few hours, so long as she did not vomit and there were no indications of discomfort. With a combination of breastfeeding and tube feeding, there is a risk of over feeding her sensitive gut.

Breastfeeding was a huge win for us, even if it was just for a few minutes. It facilitated bonding we missed during those months when she was living in the slow cooker, but it also created a problem. Knowing the joy of flavor and texture and not being able to have it on demand has made her a monster.

We are sitting in the lobby waiting to see the new gastroenterologist I chose upon Margot's discharge. Our pulmonologist also operates out of this office. They are the same gastroenterologist and pulmonologist who saw my daughters in the NICU, and I love coming here because they are always so proud. The medical assistant weighs and measures Margot and we wait for our doctor, a lovely man who speaks Arabic-accented English. He listens carefully to my concerns and my ideas; he trusts me to be my daughters' fiercest advocate.

He takes Margot from me, impressed with her weight gain since she left the NICU just a week ago. Margot turns her head to his chest and starts rooting, looking for the source of breast milk. He laughs and asks me if she's always like this. I tell him she is desperate to nurse. I report I've been following the orders not to let her stay on the breast for more than a few minutes every few hours. I all but beg him to let me feed my hungry child. He looks at her and then at me, and he tells me he doesn't want to miss this opportunity. Many babies like Margot have no will or energy to feed. Many babies like her don't like the taste and feel of breast milk or formula. He listens to me. We are collaborating to heal my daughter. He instructs me to take her off her g-tube feeds during the day, as long as I promise to get 45-60 milliliters of breast milk into her every 90 minutes to two hours.

Seven days ago, when we left the hospital, I was told to expect Margot to be on 24/7 tube feeds at least until her first birthday. Today, The Collaborator gives me permission to wean her tube feeds. I could hug him, but COVID is still raging, so I play it cool with a thank you.

I get home and disconnect Margot from the feeding pump and her portable oxygen tank. I attach her to the 50-foot tubing that connects to the oxygen condenser, a noisy machine that makes oxygen for her when we're home. For the first time in her life, I hold her and I walk without rolling an IV pole alongside us. A tangle of oxygen tubing drags on the floor behind us. At the sound of her first hungry cry, I pull out the newborn scale I've been storing under the couch in the living room. I weigh her: nine pounds, nine ounces. I unhook the flap of my nursing bra and take my daughter to my breast. For 20 minutes, she ravenously draws milk out before falling asleep. There is milk pooled in the corners of her mouth and more dripping down her chin. I smile.

I place my sleeping daughter back on the infant scale: nine pounds, eight ounces. The smile on my face turns to panic. This is how I'm supposed to gauge how much milk Margot has with each feed: weigh the baby, feed the baby, weigh the baby again. She definitely ingested milk over the last 20 minutes, but the scale says she didn't. The adage says that numbers don't lie—and maybe they don't—but the way we collect numbers is fallible. Maybe Margot lost weight from the exertion of nursing, or maybe I nudged the scale when I sat down on the couch and a two-degree change in its location threw the scale off by an ounce. Maybe she farted while she was eating and relieved herself of a benign 33 milliliters of gas. Maybe this missing ounce matters, but maybe it doesn't.

Breast feeding feels like it should be the ultimate ambition. It facilitates bonding and boosts the gut microbiome. It is supposed to be beautiful and spiritual. I stopped breast feeding Vivienne because I was at the hospital with Margot all the time. When Margot came home, Vivienne didn't want to go back to the boob. She got used to the instant gratification of a bottle, but I still have a chance with Margot. I can do this if I want to, but I don't want to. A bottle ensures I know how much milk is going into my daughter's body. A bottle will give me peace. It will make me a better mother. Letting her suck an indeterminable amount of milk from my body in the name of wholesome mothering will almost certainly require increasing my dose of Zoloft. I choose my sanity. I choose the bottle.

A week flies by, and I'm sitting in the same room with The Collaborator. Margot is fatter and happier, and her poop is not quite so watery anymore. For the first time in her life, it's more yellow sludge than yellow water. The Collaborator is floored. "This is amazing," he tells me. "She is amazing, and you are amazing." *Thank you, kind sir. You, too, are amazing.* Two weeks after the conversation in the hospital about Margot spending at least five more months on 24/7 tube feeds, The Collaborator says he doesn't think we need the feeding tube anymore, not even at night.

This is not what usually happens when a baby is born 17 weeks too early. This is not what usually happens when a baby has half a dozen surgeries before she's even supposed to be born. This is not what usually happens when a baby spends the first seven and a half months of her life in a hospital. But it's what's happening now, and for the first time in a while I don't feel survivor's guilt. I don't wonder why God gives some people miracles and others darkness and death. I soak up my miracle. I let myself be overjoyed, and I swat away the shadow that has loomed over our victories for so long. I thank God for making me the kind of mother who speaks up for her hungry baby.

The first couple of months after the girls were born, I was useless, lest one thing: I was producing milk. I may have hated the lactation consultant, but she was right about pumping consistently to make my milk come in. Pumping was the only thing I could do for my daughters in those early days, so I pumped until milk finally started flowing. I took supplements for pumping mothers. I power pumped—a practice that mimics cluster feeding and (supposedly) stimulates milk production. I sat with a book on my lap and used the pump in 15-minute increments for an hour or two every night. I carried a gallon-sized water jug around with me and made failed attempts to finish it every day. By the time the girls were two months old, I upgraded from two-ounce bottles to four-ounce bottles.

I bought a portable pump so I could pump on my way to the hospital and not miss spending time with my daughters. I woke up every two hours in the middle of the night to do my one important job, sometimes falling asleep with the machine still milking me. I would wake up with bleeding nipples and a milk-soaked nightgown. I wore that like a badge of honor. I was proud that, while I could not carry my babies to term, my body did this one thing right.

The month before Vivienne was discharged, I dropped milk off in the NICU, and the ladies in the milk room told me I had a lot of milk back there. They were wondering if maybe I could take some home. The twins had spent so many days unable to eat that I had amassed thousands of ounces of milk. When we finally brought it all home, we filled 25 cubic feet worth of deep freezers to the brim with nourishment from my body.

When I was growing up, bowel movements were never a topic of conversation in our household. No one concerned themselves with what was coming out of anyone else's butt. I gathered it was impolite to discuss such personal topics, but it shouldn't be. The consistency, color, and smell of stool tell us a great deal about our health. Margot's sludgy, yellow poop tells me she's not absorbing all her nutrients. Vivienne's very dark poop that comes out in little nuggets tell me she's constipated and maybe getting too much iron from her vitamins. Brown stool that comes out easily and leaves the toilet paper mostly clean is the holy grail of bowel movements. This is what we're going for. We're a long way off for both girls.

I was prepared to cure all my daughters' tummy troubles with the lifetime supply of breast milk. I hoped liquid gold could turn sludgy, yellow diarrhea into formed, brown poop. But today, just days after I was granted permission to feed my daughter exclusively by mouth, I am sitting on my bed watching Margot projectile poop across my white bed sheets and onto her father who is a good two feet away. It is impressive, and it's discouraging.

Jerod changes his clothes and strips the bed. I fill a syringe with Imodium. The minty, blue liquid is a six-times-a-day ritual for us. It leaves Margot's lips stained, so we've taken to calling her Imodi-lips. We try to find humor in the 10 or 12 blowouts we have to clean up every day. We try to remember how desperately we wanted our baby to poop in a diaper instead of a bag, but this isn't what I'd hoped. It's not the inconvenience of a dozen outfit changes a day that gives me anxiety; it's the future. *Will it always be this way? Will I be able to potty train a child who defecates with such urgency? Will she live her whole life worrying about where the nearest restroom is?* And then I think about Vivienne. *Is she destined for a lifetime of constipation? Will she feel bloated and uncomfortable and hate wearing bathing suits?* "Maybe I should believe..." this can get better, but I can't stop thinking about what happens if it doesn't.

I'm grateful for the bi-weekly visits with The Collaborator. It gives me some peace to know there are checks and balances to ensure my bowel movement monitoring is up to par. This week, he sends me to get bloodwork for Margot. He wants to make sure she's getting all her nutrients now that we're not using the tube. As the phlebotomist pricks my daughter and draws her blood, I am saddened by how calm she is. She's had more needle pokes than bottles of milk. Most of the time, I let myself forget this. I embrace the normalcy of bottles and bath time. I write my chronic anxiety off as just another part of keeping the babies alive, but when I'm sitting in waiting rooms or watching Margot's blood fill vial after vial, I feel robbed of something.

My friends' babies don't have to have blood drawn. They don't have to hold their kids down while an ophthalmologist sticks a speculum in their eyes. Sometimes I am overwhelmed with gratitude; other times, resentment wins. I have been working on the coexistence of opposing emotions in therapy since before Vivienne came home. Back then, Vivienne's discharge and Margot's critical condition were the reasons for my conflicting emotions. Today's catalyst is normal motherhood versus the diarrhea diaries. There are days when I get to savor how normal it is to hold my babies on my couch in my home. And there are days when I resent the poking and the prodding. I want to get home and sit in my rocking chair with my girls like a regular mom.

Is motherhood ever regular, though? We plan and pray for full-term, healthy kids, and even if we get them, they will still skin their knees and bust their lips open. They will refuse to go to sleep or will lie awake crying in the middle of the night for hours on end. They may need teeth extracted or tubes in their ears. I think of my mother who raised me to love and honor myself and to follow Jesus. Instead, I chose a treacherous path. I stumbled over every rock and fell off the occasional ledge. It was "normal" but it wasn't what she was going for.

We all come into motherhood wanting for ourselves and for our children. As our babies turn into toddlers, then big kids, teenagers, and adults, we will want different things—bigger, more complicated things—for the people we raise. None of us will get everything we want, but some of us will get closer than others. Some of us will get Harvard grads and grandbabies; others will get watery diarrhea.

CHAPTER NINETEEN

Ten Million Dollar Babies

Motherhood is exhausting. People take one look at us and they see we are the unslept, unwashed keepers of the world's future leaders or the world's future delinquents, depending on the day. Even if there were a job description for motherhood, it would never fully capture this wild gig. We could not have understood how much of our energy and our executive function it would take to keep these sprite creatures alive and intact. It is a privilege to parent if that is what one chooses, but it is also a tremendous and constant responsibility. We are even responsible for them when we are sleeping! We shouldn't be shocked by the mom who loses her mind when the toilet floods or the dentist's office calls to reschedule—again! If anything, we should wonder about the mother who doesn't.

September 2020

I have learned so much this year, like how a hospital bill for a seven and a half month stay does not come as one bill, but as separate bills for every touchpoint.

Some of the bills are from the hospital, like the rent for the space you took up there. Some of the bills are from staffing organizations that employ the physicians who work at the hospital. The bill for the MRI comes from a different place than the rest of the bills. If there's no problem—that is to say, if health insurance does what it's supposed to do—you may never notice the breakdown of your bill. If the world works the way it's supposed to, you should never find yourself surprised by ten million dollars worth of hospital bills. But when does the world ever work the way it's supposed to?

There is a problem with the bills for the twins' NICU stay. We are just finding out about it because no one started billing us until the girls were discharged from the NICU. The physician groups that have tried to bill our insurance have started calling me and sending letters to inform us our insurance has denied the claims because we were insured under another health plan.

The twins were born in December 2019 under one insurance policy; in January 2020, my employer switched insurance companies. When I found out about the change, I requested an early copy of our new insurance cards. I provided a copy of these cards to the hospital on December 31st, 2019 because I am a responsible adult like that. I did my job and I didn't think about it again.

Upon first glance at the denial letters, it appeared our providers were just billing the wrong insurance company. Our providers were asking our 2019 insurance company to cover our 2020 bills. We called each provider to explain the situation. They were all very nice about it and said they would bill the 2020 insurance company, but the 2020 insurance company also denied the claims on the basis that we were insured under another health insurance plan. *Perfect. Great. Super cool. If you could just tell me who you think was covering us, maybe we could chat with them? Maybe they could pay these bills?*

Jerod and I have spent over two dozen hours on the phone trying to find an explanation for the ten million dollars of denied NICU claims that are going to make us victims of the American healthcare system. Everything is going just as we expected.

Customer service is customer service, whether it's ten million dollars or ten dollars at stake. After a roughly 130-hour hold time, they answer the phone and tell you they will be happy to help. You begin the call by explaining this isn't your first call; you know you need to speak to a supervisor. No matter how many times you've called, they always ask you to explain your situation again. They say they want to make sure no one missed anything during the other 72 and a half million phone calls before this one, but you know they just can't be bothered to read the show notes. And once you've explained the problem you've called about 72 and a half million times, they will tell you they can't do anything about it. They will ask to put you on a brief hold while they talk to their supervisor. The supervisor will come on the line and ask you to start again from the top.

My phone is ringing. It's the ophthalmologist's office. We have an appointment in two hours. I already got a call reminding me of the appointment, so this is about something else. We do the dance where she asks me if I'm the mother of Vivienne and Margot Freeland. She pronounces the silent "t" at the end of Margot's name. I correct her; she tells me, "but there's a 't' at the end," like I'm not the one who put it there. I want to sit across from her and write *depot, escargot, and Merlot* on a piece of paper and ask her to read these words to me. I pine for a little chat about etymology and how, since the dawn of English in the 5th century, we've borrowed words from other languages, including *French* where a "t" at the end of a word is silent with very few exceptions. Instead, I say a prayer for the Florida Public School System.

The woman on the other end of the line tells me my daughters have an outstanding balance, a collective $17,000. The doctor will not see us today if we don't reconcile the account. I take a long, exasperated breath. I start from the top:

"My daughters were born in December of 2019 under one insurance policy," I explain. I talk quickly, as to not waste my time or hers.

"The company I worked for switched policies on January 1st, 2020," I continue, my voice monotonous. I know she doesn't want to hear this anymore than I want to tell it.

"Your office is likely billing the wrong insurance company," I conclude.

She tells me they are not billing the wrong insurance company. She says I need to get this bill paid or I need documentation from the insurance company that the payment is on the way. If I can't provide either of those two things, they can't provide services.

"Ok. Please hold our appointment. I will call the insurance company now." I sigh extra loud, and I hope she understands my sigh to mean I have been through enough. I hope she will have mercy on me when I show up at our appointment in an hour.

NOT WHAT I HAD IN MIND

I know the insurance companies' phone numbers by memory now. I hit zero a dozen times hoping for a transfer to something with a pulse. One minute turns to five; by the time a half hour has passed, I am so angry that hot tears are trickling down my face. I am even angrier when an upbeat woman asks if she can help me. The only thing more enraging than being on hold for 42 minutes at a time is telling this saga again knowing she's not going to be able to help me. I tell her anyway, and I ask to talk to someone who can pay the bill right now—or at the very least, someone who can give me some kind of documentation that says they will pay the bill. I beg her to help me. My daughters must see the eye doctor today.

Retinopathy of prematurity (ROP) is a condition in which abnormal blood vessels grow in the retina. Both of my daughters were treated for ROP in the NICU. The ophthalmologist follows them to make sure it doesn't come back. If it were to come back, and if it were to go untreated, they would lose their vision. As if one risk factor for blindness were not terrifying enough, my babies have high myopia that puts them at risk for retinal detachment, which would also render them blind. This is not your quotidian trip to the eye doctor to add a skosh of magnification to your prescription. My daughters' quality of life is at stake.

The Peppy Rep says she will escalate this to a supervisor who will call me back later. I know this tango.

"I've spent 24.25 hours on the phone with insurance companies over the last two months, and no one has ever called me back. I assure you, today is not the day you're going to start calling people back, Peppy. I'll wait," I scoff.

"I totally understand," she responds, and I crack.

I am sitting on my favorite chair in the house, an emerald green mid century modern office chair I bought when I turned the formal living room in our house into an open office. When you walk into our house, there are floor to ceiling bookshelves organized by color into a rainbow. There is a seating area with a plush pink chair and a royal blue ottoman—all velvet with gold hardware. I designed a double desk from a piece of natural wood counter top supported by a pair of sawhorses and a pair of filing cabinets. It's my favorite place in the house. Most of the time I love that it's right there in the open, across from the dining room, adjacent to the family room, but right now, as I start to sob and scream into the phone, I wish I had chosen a more private space for an office.

My father, my mother, my aunt, and my daughters are steps away from me when I roar into the phone.

"You do not understand. You. Do. Not. Understand. Your children have never been denied medical care that could prevent them from going blind because, even though you have insurance, no one wants to pay their hospital bill."

My throat is raw. My mother is fighting back tears. My daughters are crying because they're scared of me. I step outside, expecting this to escalate. I can't believe The Peppy Rep has the audacity to tell me she's sorry after my scathing monologue, but she does.

She clicks and clicks on her keyboard, and she tells me Margot's date of birth on the insurance policy does not match the date of birth the ophthalmologists' office submitted. She has December 15, 2019 as both girls' date of birth. I tell her this is wrong. I dart inside to grab the original paperwork we faxed to the insurance company when we added the twins to our plan. I explain I have the document in front of me, and it clearly says Margot was born on December 17, 2019.

"But you said they were twins, didn't you?" She asks.

I step outside again, and I don't hide my disdain when I tell her, "Well it would be impossible to have two babies two days apart if they weren't twins, wouldn't it?"

"Wow," is all she can muster.

I continue, "I was there. I know what happened. I know when it happened. I didn't make this mistake. Someone else did! Someone over there took the liberty of changing my daughter's date of birth. You need to take the liberty of fixing it. Now. Right now."

She tells me she can't just change it. The authorized HR representative at my former employer has to call to confirm when my daughter was born. Despite how asinine this is, I tell her I will call them right now on my way to the eye doctor, but I just need some kind of documentation to give the doctor's office to show them I am actively working to resolve this. She tells me she's sorry, but she can't do that.

I pace my front porch and shout, "You are not sorry. You are reading a script. Listen to yourself. You have no empathy. You're going to let this insurance company—a company that insured me at the time of the bills in question—ruin my life. This may not be your fault, but you are not helping."

She asks if she can place me on hold. My father, who is accompanying me and the twins to the doctor, turns the ignition of my car. My car picks up the Bluetooth on my phone at the exact time The Peppy Rep comes back, so I can't hear her because I'm on the front porch with my phone up to my ear, and she is playing through the car's stereo. By the time we figure out what's going on, The Peppy Rep has found an opportunity to flee my rage. She hangs up.

My parents and my aunt say nothing about my inability to control my emotions. My father and I buckle the twins into their seats. We get in the car. We drive two towns over to the eye physician's office in silence.

I arrive with newfound poise, and explain to the woman at the registration desk that someone at the insurance company changed my daughter's date of birth because they simply could not believe twins could be born on different days. The discrepancy between what they recorded and Margot's actual date of birth resulted in a denial of all Margot's claims. I do not mention that I have no explanation as to why Vivienne's claims have also been denied, but this 20-something with black curly hair and enormous lash extensions does not care about my insurance saga. This is a problem for the billing department. She goes to find another curly black-haired woman, and I explain everything again.

She responds with an empathetic nod and says, "that's insurance for you. I'll make a note of it on your account. And wow, twins born two days apart. I've never heard of that."

I press my lips together and close my eyes. I think, *You haven't heard the half of it, lady*, but I have the self-control this time to just say, "yeah, crazy, right?"

We see the ophthalmologist. When it's Vivienne's turn to have her eyes examined, she kicks and screams. She feels more like a college wrestler than an infant who weighed just over one pound at birth. Margot follows her sister's lead and fights so hard that I'm caught off guard by her strength. The doctor's assistant has to help me hold her down. I hate these appointments. I hate the way the doctor uses a speculum to hold their eyes open. I hate the force I have to use to hold them down. I hate the way they scream. I resent everything about this experience from the insurance meltdown to the news that their vision is getting worse. I hold this resentment in one hand and gratitude in the other because all retinas are intact and all blood vessels are as they should be. Their glasses may be thicker than their thighs, but they can see.

In the warehouse of my mind, shelves are haphazardly stacked with denied insurance claims. The birthdate mishap may have been the story I needed to get my daughters in to see the doctor today, but it's not the whole story. Only one kid's date of birth was wrong, but both kids' claims are being denied. There's not a Peppy Rep on the planet who can explain why, and without an explanation, I will keep getting bills and calls.

The stress sometimes wakes me in the middle of the night. I can't fall back to sleep because my brain won't stop trying to organize the shelves. There is a missing piece to these denial letters. If I could just find it before the phone rings again, I can stop the call from happening. I can stop myself from falling over the edge.

To anticipate ledges from which we might fall is a solid plan, but what happens when the next person finds herself slipping in that same spot? What happens when the next person is our adult child fighting their own battle against health insurance giants? If we work around the pitfalls of a broken system—be it healthcare, judicial, prison, or education—but we don't fight to reform it, what kind of world are we leaving behind for our kids? But if we fight every broken system, we will be too busy to kiss boo-boos and roast potatoes for dinner. We will be too tired for bedtime stories or early morning swim meets. This is the mess of motherhood: if we try too hard to make the world better, we may miss out on making our children better, but if we don't rally against that which is broken, future generations don't stand a chance.

CHAPTER TWENTY

Therapy: It Does a Mother Good

Historically, and across many cultures, mental illness has been tied to the supernatural. It was viewed as a spiritual problem. People speculated the mentally ill were possessed by demons or they weren't religious enough. In some religious communities, mental illness is still seen that way. Some people still believe if you're anxious or depressed, you're not trusting God enough. Most people are shocked by this gross disregard of science, but I'm not. All over the world obstetricians tell their patients that 22-weekers can't survive because that's what 20-year-old research says. Old news and fake news run rampant. If we want the best for ourselves and our families, we have to do the research and the work.

October 12, 2020

A box as tall as me—and at least twice as wide—arrived at our house today. It was so big I needed help to bring it inside. The side of the box said BOB, as in the company that makes top-of-the-line jogging strollers. I did not order this, and I'm not sure I know anyone who would send such an extravagant gift.

Now that Margot is off g-tube feeds and off the oxygen, it almost feels easy to leave the house. I've started walking, even jogging, with the girls, but our stroller wasn't designed to make turns at a 10-minute-mile pace. A couple of months ago, I made some posts on social media inquiring if anyone had a double jogger they were looking to part with. I ended up buying a decade-old, once-luxury jogging stroller for $30. It was so beat up and dirty my father did not want me to put his grandchildren in it.

It's not that we can't buy a fancy jogging stroller, there are just wiser ways to spend our money—like saving for the ten million dollars we may owe the hospital. (We're still anxiously awaiting a verdict on who will foot the NICU bill.) And what if I don't keep running? I can't imagine spending hundreds of dollars only to find out I don't really have the motivation to run, let alone push two toddlers while I'm doing it. Thirty dollars seems like a good way to test my resolve without spending money we should save for medical bills or college.

Months of pushing my daughters around the neighborhood has revealed the toll trauma has taken on me. We don't live on a busy street, but we also don't have sidewalks, so I am hyper aware of my surroundings. I wave at anyone who turns down our street to make sure they see the woman pushing two precious lives in a stroller. Whenever we get to a busy road, instead of crossing, I have visualized the many ways we could get hit by a car and die there. This also happens when I'm driving. At intersections, I quadruple check to make sure no one has failed to stop at the red light. Even after I've checked half a dozen times, I brace myself to be t-boned as I drive across the intersection.

Right before Vivienne was discharged, I started seeing a therapist. I wasn't sure how the NICU would mess me up, but I was sure it already had. A friend of a friend, a fellow micro preemie mom, shared that she had seen a licensed mental health counselor who specialized in traumatic birth after her daughter came home. She didn't want to overstep, but she didn't want me to suffer unnecessarily when she had a resource that could help. I made the call that day, and I've been seeing the Moms' Therapist ever since.

Working with her has made me more aware of how I see the world. I am irrationally and almost constantly worried that, after everything we've been through, I will be the one to kill my daughters. The anxiety is sometimes so intense it takes everything I have to get up, get dressed, and mother my children. I may read books about bettering my daughters' gut health, but I am too exhausted by my emotions to actually cook. I don't work outside our home anymore. The girls' underdeveloped lungs wouldn't survive the onslaught of respiratory illnesses found at daycare, and even if a full-time nanny made sense, I can't stomach being away from my daughters any more than I already have been, so we decided I would be a homemaker. But I am not really making a home.

I have a lot of ideas about dinner, but I cannot muster the organization and energy it takes to turn ideas into actual food. Similarly, I have neither the organizational capacity nor the will to manage the twins' ever-growing collection of clothing and toys. I am agitated, and hostile, and anxious. I am wholly disinterested in cooking, writing, or bathing—all of which used to be some of my greatest pleasures. I am unwell.

My husband and my parents know I'm unwell because they all live here. They see periods of productivity where I take my daughters to doctors' appointments and I cheer them on in physical therapy, and they see how unmotivated I am afterward, almost nonfunctional. They are all very kind. They pick up the slack I leave in my wake. They buy the groceries; they cook and they wash the dishes. They bathe Margot when she has a blowout. My father purées three dozen different vegetables every other week to diversify my daughters' gut microbes. My mother raises my babies. My husband does the laundry.

I sit in the oversized, uncomfortable rocking chair in the nursery holding my daughters, and I cry. I cry because I am so happy they are here, and I cry because I am so scared of how fragile life is. Vivienne and Margot don't mind that I'm sad, and scared, and snotty-nosed. They fall asleep on my chest, and my mom comes to set them in their beds for a nap.

I go to my bedroom. I take my antidepressant, and I dial into my video session with the Moms' Therapist. I tell her that even though I was there, I don't feel like what happened in that NICU happened to me. We've been talking about my hostility, my fears, and my inability to do the most basic tasks for months, but we haven't talked about the trauma that made me like this—at least not in a productive way.

When I talk about how my daughters came into this world and all the things that tried to kill them, I tell the story as though it happened to someone else. I am disconnected from what it felt like to see their tiny bodies in boxes. When I talk about what happened to us, I regurgitate the facts from the discharge summaries. I felt hopeless, grief-stricken, scared, and sad, but I didn't let myself sit in the gravity of our circumstances because I wouldn't have survived if I had. My brain protected itself by blocking out the desperation, and it blocked some of my memories too.

The Moms' Therapist recommends Eye Movement Desensitization and Reprocessing (EMDR), a psychotherapy treatment created to ease the anguish associated with traumatic memories. During this therapy, clients revisit traumatic memories. They uncover negative beliefs about themselves that stem from that memory and they work to formulate a new, positive belief to replace it.

I was skeptical about this course of treatment. I believe in therapy. I wouldn't have made that first appointment if I didn't, but turning negative beliefs into positive ones while my eyes flit back and forth seemed unlikely to repair my brokenness. But I didn't want to miss any more of my daughters' lives, so I was willing to try.

In almost every traumatic memory I have of my time in the hospital, my belief about myself was that I was helpless. For the EMDR to be effective, I had to formulate a new, positive belief about myself for each targeted memory. *I am a good mother. I am here for my daughters. I am strong. I am resilient. I am an advocate.*

Armed with this new perspective, we revisited the memories again while the Moms' Therapist had me follow her finger from side to side with my eyes. When she was done, she checked in with me. She asked me to revisit the memory again and rate how distressing it felt.

We did this over and over with the same memory, until it didn't feel so distressing anymore. We did it again with the next memory and the next.

We started EMDR on the things I remembered easily, like the dozen vaginal exams I had during my five-day stay at the hospital and the first time I saw Vivienne's wounds from the aspergillus infection. We used EMDR for memories that still enraged me all these months later, like the mom on the 11th floor who complained to me about spending three whole weeks in the NICU.

I revisited the alcoves of my psyche, and I saw myself from the outside. The EMDR was very effective in helping me develop empathy for myself. The new me—a mother of twins, an advocate, a relentless researcher—watched another version of myself experience complicated and traumatizing moments. I saw the lack of control I had over my body. I had no choice but to let everyone poke and prod and see the most intimate parts of me, while I waited to find out if my babies would live another hour. At the beginning, I didn't understand what was happening with my daughters. I was overwhelmed. I couldn't fathom how the gaping wounds on Vivienne's back would ever heal. I was jealous of people who wanted to love and hold my babies because, in my mind, they would be taking something away from me. People who were too hopeful or had normal thoughts about normal life made me feel invisible. Could they not see my world was turning to dust all around me? How dare they dream of a world in which everything is OK?

Upon closer inspection, they couldn't see my world collapsing because I maintained composure. With my eyes moving back and forth between my therapist's hands, I traveled back in time to these gut-wrenching moments. In the sterile room with the floor-to-ceiling windows that always had the curtains drawn, I saw the wounds, and I felt nausea rising. But there was another me there—the present version of myself who knew what my daughters and I would overcome.

We are so much stronger than I believed we were. I know how alone this mother of tiny twins felt. She tried so hard to remain standing when everything in her wanted to fall into a heap. In this strange place that was emotionally real, yet not reality, I stood next to my past self with my arm around her shoulder and told her it's OK to lose your shit, and it's OK not to. It's OK to be angry, and it's OK to be scared, and it's OK to feel alone. But you are not alone. This rendition of motherhood is dismal, and it felt like no one understood. From this new vantage point, I notice how many mothers stood with me in this fight for my daughters' lives. I couldn't see it yet because the trauma was blinding and I felt helpless, but I am as resilient as they come.

Week after week, we did this dance where my eyes followed her finger. In my mind, I held my own hand and supported myself through these traumatic vignettes. Week after week, I chose to see the best in myself. I chose to extend empathy. Sometimes I got there quickly. Other times, I couldn't access the memory or I couldn't find anything positive to believe about myself.

Even now, after all this work, sometimes I can't separate the mother I've become from the NICU mom just trying to survive. Occasionally, I'm still a powerless parent expending all my energy just to stay upright. Regardless of how I feel, I get up, get dressed, and I try to focus on treasuring the daughters I almost didn't get to raise. Healing has been slow, but it's happening.

Today, as I open the BOB box, I cannot believe someone would gift this to us. But, indeed, inside is a brand new, double wide, top-of-the-line jogging stroller. It is beautiful, and clean, and safe. It comes with a note that reads: *Thank you for sharing your story. Enjoy running with those beautiful miracles.* It's signed *a friend of a friend.*

A friend of a friend is a stranger. This extravagant gift is the kindness of someone I've never even met—someone who isn't seeking recognition for their generosity. This is overwhelmingly altruistic. I cry as I cut the plastic ties off the stroller, and I cry as I buckle the girls into it. I cry a lot lately, like everything I should have felt over the last 10 months is finally coming to the surface, and along with the ugly stuff comes an outpouring of gratitude and pure happiness.

I load my daughters into the new stroller and I lace up my running shoes. I step out into the first taste of Florida fall and I put one foot in front of the other until I'm moving at a brisk jog. For a moment, I'm not worried about cars turning onto our street because I'm reveling in a stranger's benevolence and in this body—once cut open, and now strong.

When I reach the busy street, I think about the million ways we could die, but today, it's not distressing like it was just a few weeks ago. It's not paralyzing. I can see it for what it is—a byproduct of difficult days—and I can cross the street anyway. I can imagine a day when I will be able to cross the street or drive across an intersection without the anticipation of a fatal car accident. I am on the precipice of better days.

CHAPTER TWENTY-ONE

Papá Eats Plants

We cannot control people. We cannot force them to think the way we think or feel the way we feel. It's the single most frustrating part of marriage and child rearing. We can teach our children how to treat people and we can serve our families leafy greens and lean protein for dinner, but we cannot dictate their behavior. We cannot eat their kale for them. Our kids will bite their siblings and our spouses will push the tofu to the side of their plates. Part of learning to live in relationship with others is modeling behavior and letting go of what you cannot change.

September 2020

When I met Jerod, I had been a cook-from-scratch vegetarian for nearly a decade, whereas his version of home cooking consisted of heating pre-cooked sausage in a pan of store-bought pasta sauce and serving it over spaghetti. He didn't think he liked Brussels sprouts, or sweet potatoes, or butternut squash. Though he was not entirely sure he had ever tried the latter. *Who doesn't like sweet potatoes? Surely, he just doesn't know what he likes.* Since he didn't really cook, and I love to cook, I was happy to take on the job when we got married. But a week or so into the gig I learned that every meal I made was *not his favorite*. Jerod is a polite man, never wanting to burden anyone with his preferences. When he swallowed his red lentil dal, tilted his head to the side, and told me it was not his favorite, he was really saying, "I hate this."

I am not one to accept defeat. I needed to prove to my new husband that I was a great cook—not because I had some archaic societal standard, but because it's a fact. I made him Instant Pot butter chicken from *The New Yorker*. I made pork chops in a blue cheese and white wine sauce. I made sous vide eggs and sous vide steaks. I broke a decade of vegetarianism to dine alongside him—each tiny bite of poultry was an olive branch extended to my new husband with the hope of building new habits.

His love of restaurant food kept my dear husband from seeing the peace offering. Instead, he let me know when food was "too spicy," "too dry," or, "not quite right." *Who are you, Goldilocks? You've got a lot of opinions for a guy who just gets to show up to the meal.*

After at least 50 new dishes, none of which satisfied him the way burgers and fries could, I cried at the dinner table. I cried about how we could not raise our family on Publix rotisserie chicken and plain rice. I cried about how his chronic stomach problems would never heal on a steady diet of burritos and soda, and I wondered aloud what kind of life he had led that even the very best of the *Smitten Kitchen* did not impress him.

My husband's dissatisfaction with my homemade meals did not stem from some kind of culinary elitism.

NOT WHAT I HAD IN MIND

Quite the contrary, he had spent his adult life thus far eating fast-casual takeout in his car. It took the salt of a thousand tears for us to make sense of our feelings that night. The whole grains topped with a medley of lovingly diced vegetables were an improvement from his usual fare. He didn't deny this, but that wasn't what he wanted that day. He wanted tacos, and the day before he had wanted chicken sandwiches. For 16 years, he had eaten whatever he craved, whenever he craved it. He did not plan his meals for the week on Monday because how could he know what he would feel like eating on Thursday?

Jerod is a fiscally responsible man who would not argue in favor of raising our family on restaurant food, but he wasn't ready to venture into the land of cruciferous vegetables or farmers' market kimchi. I asked him if there were any vegetables he actually liked, and he told me he liked corn. *Corn?* I thought. *You mean the most genetically modified vegetable of all time that is so worthless it comes out of your body whole?* Ok, maybe it's not worthless, but unless we're heading into the apocalypse, it's not making any superfood lists this season. I pursed my lips and closed my eyes as I worked to draft a proposal in my mind. I knew when I married him I wasn't going to change him, but I didn't imagine "'til death do us part," would be an early death, brought on by his negligible fiber consumption. This had to be negotiable.

My always-wise friend, Kelli, worked for a pediatrician's office for over a decade. She once told me it takes 27 exposures for a child to like a new food. Sometimes the first 12 exposures are needed just to get them to put the food in their mouths. Jerod is a good man. He never meant to cause me distress over dinner. He loves me more than he hates greens, and he likes me more than he likes corn; so we came to an agreement: the 27 Exposures Rule. He would try a new food 27 times before he developed an opinion about it. He promised to swap, "I don't think I like that" with "I haven't tried that enough times."

Two years later, we are sitting at our dining room table eating portobello mushroom burgers with baked sweet potato fries. Jerod still loves a good medium burger or fried chicken sandwich, but we never made it to 27 exposures before he realized he'll eat almost anything. He enjoys Indian food and Ethiopian dishes. He's happily replaced Angus beef with black bean burgers, and he even eats Brussels sprouts and kimchi on occasion. He is now a believer in meal planning and increased vegetable consumption.

I am so proud of him, but there's something we need to talk about. For our daughters to thrive, we need to take our approach to food and nutrition to the next level—a level that is, by normal standards, extreme. I am hopeful about the conversation I am going to have with my husband tonight, but I am nervous. Our daughters will be a year old in just a few months. We will transition them from a diet of mostly breast milk to a diet that's mostly real, solid food. This as an opportunity to help heal their bellies.

When Margot first came home from the hospital, a friend of mine sent me a link to an interview that podcaster and vegan ultra-endurance athlete Rich Roll did with gastroenterologist Dr. Will Bulsiewicz about the gut microbiome. She knew about the twins' complicated gut health and she thought the podcast would be helpful.

NOT WHAT I HAD IN MIND

In the way hygiene and antibiotics help people not die, the information in this interview was life-giving. This introduction to the gut microbiome became the lens through which I've thought about and researched my daughters' health. It gave me a foundation from which I can advocate for them.

Like the *micro* in micro preemie, the prefix *micro* comes from the Latin *mikros*, the Greek *smikos*, and the Proto-Indo-European root *smika*. It means small. *Biome* comes from the Greek *bios* which means life. The word *biome* refers to biological communities—colonies of bacteria that live everywhere, from deserts to bodies of water. The gut microbiome is the collective bacteria, fungi, viruses, and protozoa that inhabit our digestive system. The largest population of gut bacteria abide in the colon where they feast on the undigested fiber that remains largely intact on its journey through our intestines. While our germophobic Western culture often sees bacteria, viruses, and fungi as enemies, the good bacteria in the gut helps us break down our food; it helps us get more nutrients from what we eat.

When the good bacteria in the gut feasts on fiber from fruits, vegetables, legumes, and whole grains, they produce short-chain fatty acids which create and maintain a strong barrier between the intestines and the rest of the body, thus preventing the condition known as leaky gut. Short-chain fatty acids also protect against inflammation. They are crucial to good gut health and may help prevent diseases like cancer, asthma, and even dementia.

I have a stack of books about gut health on the dining room table next to loose papers with notes from dozens of studies I've gathered from PubMed and internet friends in the medical community. I have a mental list of what I've learned about the gut microbiome and the role of resistant starches in managing diarrhea for short-bowel patients. I have articles about the microbiome's important role in immune system health, and I'm pleading my case for how we can heal our daughters' bellies and improve their immune systems. And, as a side project, I've been researching how to live this super clean life without wrecking my daughters' relationships with food.

In a world that runs on at least double the daily recommended sugar intake, I'm asking Jerod to ditch everything he's ever deemed delicious and to model behavior for our daughters. Everything I've read about the gut microbiome says we should eat mostly plants. Meat may not hurt, but it won't help. Dairy may hurt and definitely won't help, and sugar will sabotage all our efforts.

For weeks, I've been sharing vignettes of this research with him, and for weeks he has gently pushed back. He doesn't see why it has to be so extreme. He has a feeling—backed not by scientific research, but by his chocolate-chip-pie-loving heart—that meat, dairy, and sugar will not kill our kids. I can't disagree. I know our daughters won't die if they eat the way we grew up eating. I also know we can do better than not dying. We can ditch the antidiarrheal drugs and maybe even avoid asthma. We can thrive.

He worries our kids will feel left out at birthday parties when every other kid has a face full of vanilla frosting. He doesn't want them to miss out. I bite my tongue to soothe my seething mind. We are looking at two different seasons of life. His vision is of a toddler birthday party and mine is of a teenager carrying a bag full of medication to a sleepover, or a young adult declining an invitation to dinner because it will give her diarrhea. I am pressing my husband to take the long view with me. I need him to realize our kids won't remember the cake or the ice cream they had when they were two, but they may develop a taste for sweets that will have lasting effects on their health.

I don't just need him to agree with me. I need him to help me. I doubt my ability to make 21 meals a week at home without his support. I lose sleep over this because I know if my daughters' father does not embrace root vegetables and winter squash on our dinner table, they won't either. If *papá* keeps a stash of stale cookies in the cupboard, they will know, and they will assume those are better than the lemon chia pudding I am serving them.

My stance is that we don't need to attend birthday parties until the kids are old enough to understand that frosting may light up their pleasure centers, but it will also make them sick. Now is not the time to eat fried chicken and ice cream in moderation. Now is the time to shape our daughters' preferences so when the ice cream finally comes, it's too sweet for their taste. Our daughters' medical histories are extreme; it makes sense that our approach to healing would also be.

He rolls his eyes. I stomp my feet. I concede that maybe our kids will feel left out if they aren't eating icing at a one-year-old's birthday party, but what about when they are 10 and they are the only kid at the party running to the toilet every five minutes? What happens when Margot is the only kid in class who has to take an adult-sized dose of Imodium every four hours? What if we can set aside American traditions like hamburgers, hot dogs, and free cookies at the grocery store to create a rich culture of exciting, healthy foods that will spare our kids a lifetime of anxiety about where the nearest restroom is?

I've presented my research and my plans to our pediatrician and The Collaborator. The only person I have left to convince is my husband. It's not about convincing him to feed our daughters an exclusively plant-based diet. He will not fight me over what I feed them. This is about convincing him that what he models for them matters. It's about reminding him of the power he holds to influence not just what our daughters eat, but who they become. I have a speech prepared. My husband is not surprised.

We have two tiny daughters to raise, and I want to raise them not just to eat their vegetables but to love their vegetables. I want to teach them what real food tastes and feels like. I want them to enjoy digging up carrots from the garden and eating kale right off the plant. I cannot concern myself with what you eat when you're not in the house. But I will not spend a lifetime telling our daughters that the steak or the candy bars or the potato chips you keep in the house are papá's special food. All you ever want when you're a kid is what your parents have.

I want to create a home where, when our kids want what's on our plates, we love sharing it with them because we know it's good for them—because we know it's healing. I want us to model the food choices we want our kids to make in the same way we model how we want them to behave and how we want them to treat people.

I have spent months researching and reading and talking to doctors so we can give our daughters a better quality of life, and I would really like you to trust me. I know this differs from how you grew up. I know it's not always going to be your favorite, but I also know this change can be full of exciting flavors, textures, and colors. This can be an adventure that makes all of our lives better. You can simply tolerate it and do whatever you want outside of this house, or you can get onboard.

He is silent and his affect is flat, but I see his head spinning. I wonder if I need to say more, but I have given him everything I have, and it will either move him or it won't.

He looks up, smiles, and tells me, "OK, so I guess I'm vegan now."

We cannot control people, but we can share what's on our hearts. We can provide perspective. We can model behavior. We can rage or we can take a step back. We will not stand united on every front with the people we love, but there is so much power when we stand united for the people we love.

CHAPTER TWENTY-TWO

Milestones and White Lies: A Survival Guide

If we're lucky, we will grow wise enough to stop caring what the world thinks. It won't hurt our feelings when we're not invited to the party—it may even be a relief. We will care less, or not at all, about what is trendy. Instead, we will wear clothes that make us feel comfortable or beautiful, preferably both. There comes a time when the weight of other people's expectations will no longer be a burden we care to carry. The same, unfortunately, may not always be true when it comes to the weight of people's expectations of our children.

December 2020

My daughters' first birthdays are next week. They have round bellies and thighs that almost jiggle. They laugh and babble. They are tiny for one-year-olds, and they have gross and fine motor delays, but you would never look at them and wonder why they are so damaged. They don't look like they spent the first half of their lives in an intensive care unit. They don't look like they have spent the second half of their lives in therapies to inch toward the milestones their peers achieved effortlessly.

We expect a lot from babies. These little humans come into the world naked and shocked. They have less muscle tone than an earthworm, and we presume they will hold their heads up, roll over, and push up onto all fours in due time. We trust they will move opposite hands and knees to get from one place to the other. We assume they will pull themselves up to stand and cruise along couches and coffee tables. The evolution of the brain and body is brilliant, naturally moving babies toward milestones, even when parents are too distracted to aid in the process. There are, however, always exceptions, special cases that require intervention.

Some brains and bodies are wired differently. Some brains are injured. Some bodies don't have enough muscle to hold themselves up. Some babies, like mine, spent too much time in beds instead of on their bellies. When babies don't fit into the boxes pediatricians must check, there are therapists to teach us how to work with what our children *can* do.

The word *therapy* exists in both Latin, *therapia*, and Greek, *therapeia*. In both languages, these words mean to heal, to cure, and to take care of. Every week since the girls got home, The Lioness comes over for physical therapy. She is regal and she is damn good at her job. I would say she takes no prisoners, but she literally takes my daughters captive for an hour a week. Her arrival is enough to make Vivienne and Margot cry in anticipation of the hard work awaiting them. The wailing and flailing doesn't bother me. I know what is good for us doesn't always feel good in the moment.

NOT WHAT I HAD IN MIND

The Lioness is a gift. Rumor has it she is one of the very best pediatric physical therapists in the country. She is relentless in her pursuit of strengthening my daughters' muscles and creating neural pathways where there were none. She is patient and unfazed by Margot's sludgy, yellow blowouts. She believes in my daughters.

The Lioness came to us through divine intervention. We knew Vivienne and Margot needed physical therapy, but schlepping two infants—one still on oxygen at the time—to a downtown waiting room full of grimy kids at the height of the coronavirus was daunting. Being the proactive and reasonable mother I am, I put it off. I told myself I would call the therapist when both girls were home. But by the time both girls were home, The Lioness, whose son works with Jerod, had heard our story.

Her career is well past the in-home therapy stage, but every year she hand picks a couple of babies to treat free of charge. She calls this her ministry. This year, she chose us. This is how a world-class physical therapist came to be seated on my living room floor every Friday morning.

We've replaced the rug in the living room with a padded play mat. The perimeter of the room is lined with physical therapy props: an extra large exercise ball, a baby-sized bench, and sensory brushes. These tools are on loan to us until our daughters start to walk. The Lioness has seen a lot of babies, and she believes our daughters will walk. She's told me this a dozen times, and every time I think of the OB who warned us that, even if the girls lived, they might never walk. I think about the DNR that never came and the day Margot coded, and I cry. They are joyful tears, but they contain just a hint of sadness for every mother whose babies never made it to physical therapy.

When your children survive against all odds, no one warns you about the survivor's guilt that accompanies the miracle. In public, I cry happy tears when I talk about my daughters. Online, I share photos of their brilliant fashion sense and their milestones. But in text messages, phone calls, and private messages with other moms like me, we talk about the guilt and the relief. When cancer or prematurity or car accidents take a baby's life, I experience sadness and grief accompanied by a hint of ease that it wasn't my daughters. This is followed by the sharp pang of wrongdoing. It's so twisted to feel relief in response to someone's tragedy, but I can't stop it. My therapist says to just feel it. It is not a moral shortcoming that trauma has changed the way I experience the world. She reminds me to be present with my daughter and not to let guilt steal my joy.

With some support, Vivienne is standing. The Lioness presses my daughter's feet into the ground, forcing her to feel what it's like to support her body on those ten tiny toes. She makes Vivienne support herself with her hands on the baby-sized bench, and she moves Vivienne's little hands along the bench, waiting for her feet to follow. Sometimes they follow; most of the time, my daughter cries in frustration and gives up. She plops down, the padding of her diaper providing a soft place to land. She gets over it quickly and acts as if the harrowing cruise across the bench never happened.

When it's Margot's turn, The Lioness puts my daughter belly-down on top of a big blue exercise ball. Margot does not stand yet. She doesn't even sit. Whenever we try to get her to straighten her legs and press her feet into the ground, she recoils. For now, we are focusing on core strength. Balancing her on the ball, The Lioness puts Margot's hands under her shoulders to encourage her to lift her chest off the ball. When she lifts, The Lioness rolls the ball forward, backward, and side-to-side. She wants Margot to use her abdominal muscles to stabilize herself—the same muscles that have been cut open on three occasions. It seems like too much to ask of this young body that's been through so much. Margot shakes the way I do on the rare occasion I can sneak in a core workout. She struggles and cries, and she is ultimately victorious, at least for today.

Before premature babies are two years old, their milestones are assessed according to how old they would be if they had been born when they were supposed to be. While the twins turn one next week, they would only be eight months old if they had been born on their due date. A baby who isn't crawling or sitting up at eight months old is not ideal, but it's not cause for alarm—at least not yet. The Lioness is not worried about Margot, but I am.

When Margot came home at seven-and-a-half-months old, she had no muscle tone. She was as floppy as a baby born this morning. She has followed the normal progression of a newborn baby. She's found her hands. She's learned to hold her head up and lift her chest off the ground during tummy time. She knows to put her hands on the ground to create a tripod for support when she tries to sit. She is doing everything she should be doing, but her sister is doing more, so I worry. I worry Margot won't catch up. I worry the world will wonder what's wrong with this one-year-old baby who doesn't sit up or crawl.

When the girls were still on oxygen and Margot on her continuous feeds, I never took them anywhere except the doctors' offices. The oxygen tanks and feeding pump made leaving the house overwhelming. Mostly, I was unnerved by the anticipation that an innocent kid or an ignorant adult would ask what was wrong with my daughters. I knew if someone posed such a question, I would crack. Back then, I was worried the world would see their tubes and make assumptions about who they are or what they are capable of.

We don't have tubes anymore, but I still live in fear of the questions that highlight my daughters' differences. When I load the girls into the stroller and go for long walks around the neighborhood, people always stop us to coo at them. There is something magnetic about identical twins; people cannot help but ask questions. Inevitably, someone will ask how old they are, and I lie. I adjust for prematurity and tell strangers they are eight-months-old. Sometimes, I say they are six-months-old. I tell people whatever I think they need to hear to avoid further questioning.

Everywhere we go, I evade giving an explanation for why my daughters are so tiny, why they wear glasses, or why they have deep, long scars across their bellies. In some ways, the world is getting better. We see people with all abilities in literature and on television. Having one leg didn't stop *Grey's Anatomy's* Arizona Robbins from becoming a double-board-certified fetal and pediatric surgeon. But humans are broken, and kids don't have filters to stop them from reflecting their parents' biases.

I go home and do the physical therapy exercises The Lioness ordered. I pray my kids will catch up. I pray they will be spared a lifetime of awkwardness and cruelty, and I lie as needed.

Of all the milestones my one-year-old daughters have not yet achieved, I worry the most about Margot not sitting up. I worry that maybe the MRI missed something. Maybe the right side of her cerebellum is crucial to her being able to sit up, and since it's smaller than it should be, she will lay on her belly the rest of her life. My research has yielded zero cases in which this has ever happened, but my anxiety assures me there is a first time for everything.

I sit her on the play mat. She uses her hands to create a tripod for support. I use my hands to press her hips firmly into the ground, forcing her to feel herself rooted, safe, and strong. I've put a pacifier in my mouth, in hopes she will abandon her tripod position and reach for it. The Lioness did not teach me this strategy, it's a *mamá* original. Margot reaches for the pacifier. With my support, she is confident. I pull the pacifier back. She complains. I ease up on her hips; she wobbles and tries to use her core muscles to stabilize. She can't find her balance. This is our daily work.

We wake up. We eat. We head to the play mat where Vivienne supports herself on the baby-sized bench. I put a toy or a snack on the other end of the bench to lure her into taking steps. I sit Margot on the mat, and every day I reduce how much support I'm giving her. Every day, I dangle something truly irresistible—like a bottle or a light-up rattle—in front of her to tempt her to abandon her tripod. And every time she abandons her tripod, she falls.

My brother is in town from California for Christmas. My parents want to take family photos at Lake Eola in downtown Orlando. I do not want to take family photos because I am an unslept mother of one-year-old twins and I still look a wee bit pregnant. But, since Margot's homecoming, my parents have fed me and clothed my children. They've lived in my house and done my laundry. They have gotten up to take care of my daughters in the middle of the night just as often (if not more often) as I have. So, I'm taking family photos.

I pack the diaper bag with a lifetime supply of diapers and 42 packs of wipes. I take four extra outfits for the girls and a cooler with two bottles of milk. We load the stroller and the babies and we drive 2.1 miles to the lake. My dad sets his camera atop a tripod and takes test photo after test photo to get the light just right. My mom brought white wooden letters that spell the word *familia*. She thinks she can get the girls to each hold a letter. I think she may be able to get the girls to each eat a letter, which is good enough. I sit the girls in the grass. I stand behind Margot to support her while I sort through the letters. She leans away from me and sits up. I step back. She keeps sitting, as though this is just a thing she does now. I snap a photo of my daughters sitting side by side in their red and gray knitted onesies with Peter Pan collars. There are no tubes on their faces or in their bellies. Their scars are covered with clothing and their glasses are in the diaper bag because they kept pulling them off. They look like typical eight-month-olds.

I look at the picture I took. I look back at my daughters. The picture is incomplete. It is a snippet of a beautiful life, but you can't see the depths of the beauty when you don't know how we got here. I have been so scared my daughters will be different and the world will be cruel to them that I couldn't see how my daughters' stories might be just what people need for a new perspective. My daughters' stories might be just what the world needs to believe in miracles.

CHAPTER TWENTY-THREE

The Dancing Poop Doctor: A Collaboration

Some ailments can be addressed swiftly. Acetaminophen stops the throb of a headache; a bandage stops the bleeding of a skinned knee. Conditions of the chronic persuasion, however, are not so easily remedied. Allergies, chronic diarrhea, migraines, and arthritis have to be managed with medication, diet, and lifestyle. Maybe, if we're diligent for months or years, these chronic maladies will slip into remission and remain there. The pursuit of remission can drive even an atheist to whisper an occasional plea toward heaven.

March 2021

I schedule our medical appointments around nap time and, more importantly, around poop time. To minimize the chance of having to change my clothes and Margot's in a public restroom, I aim for appointments that fall just after the morning poop extravaganza, but before nap time. I thought we would be OK for this 10:15 a.m. appointment with GI today. I thought she had gotten it all out before we left the house. But now I am in this tiny bathroom with a feces-covered child on the changing table, my gray dress wet with diarrhea—hers, not mine.

I clean my brown-eyed girl up and put her in a fresh dress—a little lemon number I got her for Easter. I always save the good clothes for after the public display of diarrhea. She vocalizes her disapproval of her place on the changing table until I sit her up. She smiles and laughs as if to tell me she is pleased with the wardrobe change. I left my wardrobe change at home today, so I'll be wearing eau de poo for the rest of the morning.

I requested this appointment because Margot's diarrhea, which had been getting better since we started her on solid foods, is back. There are plastic tubs of poo-stained clothes soaking in stain remover in my guest bathroom. The number of diapers we are going through daily is a crime against the environment and a violation of our household budget. But it's the long-term implications of this diarrhea that keep me awake. Instead of sleeping when the kids sleep, I read medical journal articles about short bowel syndrome in neonates. I search for IBD, IBS, and Crohn's disease, wondering if all this pooping is a byproduct of a problem or if all this pooping is going to create a new problem.

There are people in this world who accept what they cannot change—people without anxiety who can sleep even when something life-altering is outside of their control. I am not one of those people. Before the medical assistant measures and weighs my daughter, I already know what the numbers will be. I know she has not gained any weight the last four weeks, but she has grown taller. I know The Collaborator is not going to be worried yet because she isn't losing weight, but I'm worried, and I'm wondering if any of the research I've been doing might help us here.

Two hundred and twenty-four days in the NICU did not make me a physician, but the thousands of pages I read about the gut microbiome got me as close to an MD as I'm ever going to get. Which is to say, I'm never going to be a doctor, but I moonlight as the twins' unregistered dietitian. Despite my lack of credentials, The Collaborator always reads my research and listens to my concerns.

I suspect Margot's diarrhea is not just because she's missing 24 centimeters of her small bowel. There has to be something else going on, preferably something I have some control over, like her gut microbiome.

Vivienne and Margot were dealt a bad biome—or rather, they were dealt no biome at all. They were half-baked when they came into this world and what little gut microbiome they may have been born with was decimated by the antibiotics and anti-fungal medication that saved their lives. I want to believe Margot just doesn't have the right bacteria living in her gut yet. I need to believe I can cook my way out of this because I have what is commonly referred to as control issues.

The Collaborator doesn't disagree. He supports the fiber-rich diet void of sugar, processed foods, and dairy I've been feeding my daughters to help them feed their good bacteria. We are both hopeful we will be able to make this better with food instead of bottles of chalky, mint-flavored medication, but he is prescribing more minty chalk until we get there. Chronic diarrhea and mediocre weight gain are not alarming for a baby with Margot's history, but they are cause for more Imodium. The Collaborator adjusts her dose for her weight. He tells me we aren't going to worry yet. He wants me to keep doing what I'm doing, and he will see us back in four weeks.

An extra milliliter of Imodium every six hours while we wait for things to work themselves out is not the type of control I was going for. I want to do something. I want a superfood to slow down the diarrhea or a mix of baby-safe magic mushrooms that will populate the gut with good bacteria. I want to go home and cook a cure.

I make our appointment for next month at the checkout desk. I open all the car doors and blast the air conditioner before I buckle Margot into the car seat, and I send up a prayer against blowouts between here and home. The good Lord delivers, and when we arrive home I carry a sleeping Margot from her carseat to her crib. My mom has already put Vivienne down to nap, so I head to the kitchen to sauté not-magic mushrooms. The thought occurs to me that maybe Dr. Will Busiewicz—the gut health MD—can help. A drive to Charleston, South Carolina seems like a small price to pay for a path forward. I am optimistic about this solution for a good five minutes until the receptionist answers and tells me that Dr. Bulsiewicz does not see pediatric patients and they don't have a referral for me.

A plant-based pediatric gastroenterologist who assesses patients through the lens of the gut microbiome seems more like a wish I'll need to find a genie to grant than a real possibility, but it's worth a search. I put the mushrooms on a plate and cut them into tiny pieces with a pair of kitchen shears, and I rush to my computer to see what I can find before the girls wake up from their nap. I search for *Plant-based pediatric gastroenterologist,* and there she is: The Dancing Poop Doctor. She is the gastroenterologist of my dreams. She has huge green eyes and jet black hair, and she delights in getting patients off their meds with diet and lifestyle changes. There's just one glaring problem: New York is a much further drive than South Carolina. I send her a message on Instagram: *Do you see patients virtually?* She responds immediately, telling me to call her office and they can set me up with a virtual visit. I dial the number, make the appointment, and dance all the way back to the nursery to pick up my crying baby girls. "We are going to be OK, girls. We are going to be OK."

My calendar is a grocery list with appointments written in the margins. Our appointment with The Dancing Poop Doctor is circled and highlighted—a beacon of hope. In the three days leading up to the appointment, I stay up late into the night rereading the small library I've accumulated about the gut microbiome. I reference Margot's medical history and highlight all the gut-bacteria-killing antibiotics associated with an increased risk of IBD, ulcerative colitis, and Crohn's disease. I keep Margot's food diary 100% up-to-date and I take photos of all her poops.

It feels like Christmas morning as I wait for The Dancing Poop Doctor to log onto our call. She is everything I hoped she would be: inquisitive, supportive, encouraging, and full of possibility. She, like the doctors who came before her, believes Margot has enough bowel to poop like a healthy kid, she just needs some rehabilitation. She wants to start with one change at a time and we will reconvene every two weeks to discuss how that change has impacted her digestion.

One change every two weeks is not the pace I was hoping for, but I agree to switch Margot's toddler formula and to keep shooting the chalky mint liquid down her throat with a syringe every six hours. In the meantime, I fill out the paperwork for The Dancing Poop Doctor and The Collaborator to share information with each other—a collaboration for the sake of solid stool. He knows all there is to know about my daughter's medical history and she looks at it with fresh eyes and the possibility of rehabilitating her gut microbiome. It is rare in American healthcare to find one doctor who will wholeheartedly support you in a quest to manage chronic illness without medication. It is almost unheard of to find two doctors who will work together across state lines to make it happen. I have found favor with the Lord.

For two weeks, I keep impeccable logs of everything my daughters eat. I take pictures of poop with comments about what Margot ate to produce such ungodly bowel movements. Our family and friends laugh at us, but our doctors applaud.

On our next virtual visit, The Dancing Poop Doctor talks to me about resistant starches, which are natural stool binders and powerful supporters of a healthy gut microbiome. A resistant starch is a complex carbohydrate that doesn't get digested in the small intestine. It makes it all the way to the colon where it can feed the good bacteria. I read everything I can find about resistant starches and their effectiveness at binding stool. I learn green plantains are a top source of resistant starch, and I am delighted. This is the food of my people. Plantains in all their resistant starch glory are served with everything from Cuban breakfasts to snacks, dinner, and sometimes dessert. I was brought up on plantain purées. I was raised for a culinary job such as this.

The first time I was pregnant, Jerod and I sat on the leather couches that were too big for the 1950s bungalow he bought the year before we started dating. We stayed up until the wee hours of the morning imagining what we would name our child and what kind of parents we would be. We have different perspectives than we did back then, but there is one thing that hasn't changed. I have kept my commitment to raise Spanish-speaking children who are connected to their heritage.

Both of my parents came to the U.S. from Cuba, my mother in the early 1960s and my father in the early 1970s. My grandparents, on both sides, gave up everything they knew to give their children freedom to buy as many plantains as they needed at the grocery store and to practice their faith freely. My four grandparents stretched their budgets and their living spaces to raise six children between them. Those children grew up, went to school, and became educators and C-level executives. Some of those children had their own children: me, my brother, and my cousins.

My maternal grandfather did not live to meet most of his grandchildren, and my maternal grandmother died just three years before her great granddaughters were born. My paternal grandparents, however, have experienced the wonder of watching Vivienne and Margot evolve from one-pound fetuses into 20-pound babes who throw food on the floor and laugh about it. The girls' great grandparents are both amused and horrified when they watch this darling duo of mine spoon pureed black beans partially into their mouths. When they go to the Latin market, my grandparents always buy extra mangoes, yuca, malanga, and green plantains for my daughters.

When Vivienne was not even a year old (eight months when adjusted for prematurity) she asked for her pacifier. I was playing a game where I pulled it out of her mouth and gave it back, hoping to make her laugh. She laughed the first time, but the second time she looked at me and said, "tete." *Tete* is an abbreviation of the Spanish word for pacifier: *chupete*. Just a few weeks later, I was changing Margot's diaper when she exclaimed, "caca." My second born daughter, plagued with chronic diarrhea since she was six days old, said *poop* as her first word. The humor of this was not lost on anyone. More important than the girls' first words is the language of those first words.

People often comment about how great it is that I'm teaching my children Spanish. In their minds, it is a skill that will make them more employable in the state of Florida. But I'm not "teaching" my kids Spanish any more than my husband is "teaching" them English. I'm raising them in Spanish because Spanish is the language my family and our ancestors have spoken for hundreds of years.

My grandparents don't speak English. Margot and Vivienne are the last generation of my grandparents' legacy that they will live to know, and what a shame it would be if they couldn't understand each other. How sad would it be if we saw green plantains as just a weird food we had to eat to regulate our digestion instead of a staple of our heritage? I don't think it's a coincidence that these green bananas and the root vegetables popular in Cuba and the other islands are the perfect foods to help my daughter.

With no experience, no credentials, and no potential to publish a paper, I run a study in which no one gets a placebo and everyone gets green plantains. Within four days of starting the girls on a daily serving of half a boiled green plantain each, sliced and doused in lemon juice, Margot's yellow sludge turns into yellow clumps. Within two months, the yellow clumps turn brown. Her weight steadily increases. For the first time since she was discharged from the NICU she is growing wider faster than she is growing tall. Within three months, I only have to carry two changes of clothes, instead of six.

At our follow-up appointment with our local gastroenterologist, I am sitting on the examination table with Margot on my lap. The Collaborator has my phone, and he's scrolling through an album I created with photos of poop, Margot's poop. They are remarkable photos of brown lumps that stay together in the diaper. Sometimes the lumps are light and yellow and less than ideal. Sometimes the lumps are creamy and don't quite stay together, but the point is there are no photos of watery, yellow diarrhea here. The Collaborator tells me he did not expect such perfection to come from Margot's colon until she was much older. He is pleased. I am relieved. I share the studies I found on green plantains to manage diarrhea, and I tell him these viridescent cousins of the banana have been more effective than Imodium. He says we don't need the minty chalk anymore. He tells me her poop looks beautiful.

"Caca," Margot coos at the sound of her favorite word.

"Si, caca bella," I laugh.

PART 4:
THIS IS MY FIGHT SONG

CHAPTER TWENTY-FOUR

The End of an Era

Most of the time, life is messy. Our timing is always a little off. There are more loose ends than happy endings. But occasionally, the end of an era is so perfect, it could pass for fiction.

April 2021

Orlando sits at the center of Orange County, Florida. While the city is most famous for The Mouse, the actual rodents here once wandered freely among the groves for which the county was named. When they paved paradise and put up my neighborhood, the rats lost their homes, but the resilient little narks moved into the hedges that separate our house from the neighbors. I have been raising my babies in my home while they're been raising theirs in my backyard. Until last week, we had no idea we were squatting on Master Splinter's land.

We thought a bottle of water had spilled in the backseat of The Monster Truck. Why else would the backseat on the passenger's side be soaked? But when the damp spot wouldn't dry and it started to spread, we turned to the dealership to solve the mystery. When they called to tell us a rat had eaten through the line that drains the air conditioner, we were more concerned about where said rat had come from than we were about the damage to the car.

The Monster Truck sleeps in the garage, and apparently it's not the only thing sleeping in the garage. We are still trying to figure out if our health insurance is going to foot the twins' NICU bill, but at least we know our much-more-helpful car insurance company is definitely covering the rat damage. The dealership tells us they need time to assess the destruction and quote the repairs. In the meantime, insurance will provide a comparable rental car.

Jerod comes home early to meet the pest control man. There are rat droppings in the attic above the garage, but it appears Master Splinter was just here scavenging for food. Fortunately for us, he is not housing his second family above our garage. Unfortunately for us, making sure he doesn't make another meal of our automobiles will take four to six weeks and cost about the same as closing expenses on a new home. Thus, I've been thinking about setting our house on fire, but we leave for our first family vacation tomorrow, so that will have to wait.

The pest control guy sets traps around and above the garage. I don't know how I feel about Master Splinter's impending death. It was his land first, and if he would stick to living on the land instead of in my house, we wouldn't have any problems. But I'm not even sure how to reach him, let alone how to try to communicate with him without ending up institutionalized. I'm going to let Jerod handle this because, based on how much this is going to cost us, he's not having any ethical turmoil over murdering Master Splinter.

I put the kids to bed and pack the last of the toiletries. My head hits the pillow at eight o'clock, but I toss and turn as I anticipate our wake-up call. The girls still don't sleep through the night—a lingering effect of the interrupted sleep during their NICU time. Our plan is to leave for the mountains of north Georgia after their middle-of-the-night cup of oat milk. We are hopeful to make it at least halfway through the eight-hour drive before they wake up for breakfast.

They sleep until just before three o'clock in the morning, and at the first sound of a cry, we hand each girl her sippy cup and load them into car seats in the dark. We carry the car seats out to the rental SUV. We make it five whole hours before they wake up confused, hungry, and wet. We take the next exit, and in a gas station parking lot, we change diapers and feed babies. Before loading the family back into the rental for the rest of the drive, we swap the girls' pajamas for cute little sweaters and leggings.

The rental car is a three-row SUV with captain's seats, which makes it easy to entertain the kids from the third row. I would not be mad if we traded in The Monster Truck for something less trucky with captain's seats. I wonder aloud if maybe we should consider something more like this, and Jerod reminds me we just paid off The Monster Truck. We are not getting a new car.

When we arrive at the lake house, I feel like we should win some kind of parenting prize for making an eight-hour drive in under nine hours with twin toddlers in tow. The twins, still too young to appreciate the change of scenery, snack on green plantains while Jerod and I flip through tourist brochures and scour the internet for hiking trails and the nearest grocery store. My parents arrive a couple of hours after us, well-rested and ready to enjoy a late lunch on the lake. I'm new to this traveling-with-tiny-kids thing, but I am pretty sure the only way to do this right is to bring a set of grandparents. My parents even take Vivienne overnight, so we're only waking with Margot.

A year ago, I was wondering if Margot would need a tracheostomy; a vacation was an impossibility. Now, we're waking up in a lake house and heading out to hike. There is a two-pound weight difference between the twins, likely because Margot's missing bowel makes it a little harder for her to absorb nutrients. Those two pounds work in my favor for the two-and-a-half mile hike down to the falls. I wear Margot and Jerod wears Vivienne; the girls laugh as they bounce in their carriers. I spend most of the hike watching the ground, for fear of tripping, falling, and squashing my daughter to death.

When I get to the bottom, the even ground and the sound of rushing water relax me. I hand the baby over to my mom and make her promise not to drop her into the waterfalls, and I step back to take in the view.

The moments where we step back and observe the life we've built have a spiritual quality. I imagine God taking in the grandeur of his creation and deeming it good. Sure, I didn't design this ecosystem, nor the species that abide in it, but I had something to do with the lives in front of me. I cooked those babies, if only halfway. I made my parents parents and then grandparents. I made my husband a father. I didn't do it perfectly—I didn't even finish the job, and I put us through a lot of pain in the process—but I made them. We all made it here, and it is good.

Back at the trailhead, Vivienne and Margot sit in the gravel. They alternate between drinking milk and sucking homemade golden beet purée from reusable squeeze packs. We change their diapers in the trunk, and we wipe them down before buckling them into their car seats where they fall asleep before we've even put the car into gear.

We drive by the local hospital on the way back to the lake house. It's a single building, just four stories tall. I cannot help but wonder what we would have done if, when the twins were born, we had lived in a town like this—charming and quiet, but lacking the equipment and education to sustain babies like mine. I wonder how many pregnant mothers have walked into that hospital in circumstances far less severe than mine and left grieving the loss of their baby. I don't pretend to know why my daughters are on vacation today when so many never made it out of the hospital, but I know it was more than just luck.

My phone rings. I don't recognize the number and I don't have service on this side of the mountain anyway, so I let it go to voicemail. I daydream about what it would be like to live somewhere away from the city where we could hike and be on the water. Then, I remember the hospital. I consider the grocery store that doesn't sell tahini or tofu, and I promptly close the book on that idea.

The next few days we read books, take naps, and spend early mornings and late afternoons picking daffodils with our kids. We wanted this trip to be a retreat.

The word *retreat* has its roots in the French word *retrete*, a word that means to withdraw to a secluded place. When we think of this word in terms of a vacation, we think of a place like this, tucked in the mountains, away from the world. But *retreat* is also a military term meaning to fall back from battle. To feel safe enough to retreat to a town nearly two hours from a legitimate hospital is a sign that we did not just fall back from the battle. We won. We can rest.

Our second-to-last day at the lake house, we drive to a lookout on a mountaintop. There's a light fog obstructing the view, but it still feels like I'm on top of the world. To successfully vacation with a pair of 16-month-olds feels like the height of my parenting career. Who needs Europe when you've got Hiawassee, Georgia a mere eight hours away by car? (I'm kidding!)

On the winding drive down the mountain, the girls fall asleep. When we arrive at the lake house, Jerod rolls the windows down to let in the spring breeze. I am about to offer to stay in the car with the girls until they wake up, when his phone rings. He gives me the *I have to take this* look. I pick up my phone and listen to the voicemail from the other day. My eyes widen at the sound of what I hear, but before I can finish, the girls are stirring. I unbuckle them and do the twin mom shuffle to get one in each arm. I carry them to the door and I kick it with my foot until my dad lets me in. I am dying for Jerod to listen to the voicemail, but I find him sitting on the couch, still on the phone. He is laughing in what appears to be disbelief.

"Very funny," he says. "but no really, what's the damage?"

I realize it's the car dealership.

"No," he says drawing out the "o."

"Are you serious?" I can tell he's shocked, but I can't tell what the news is.

"Ok, I will call the insurance company now." He sighs and hangs up.

My husband looks at me and my parents. We are eagerly waiting to hear what the other side of the conversation entailed. He presses his lips together and opens his mouth; then he closes it again. He does this a couple of times before he says, "The car was deemed a total loss."

I dissolve into laughter. I insist he is not serious. He wishes he were witty enough to come up with a joke such as this, but it's just too ridiculous. The car is, in fact, a total loss. I do the mental math of what this debacle is going to cost us. But then I remember the voicemail, and I feel a wave of relief.

It was someone from the insurance company—the only person capable of solving the ten million dollar mystery we've been working on for the last eight months. He said that under the *newborn extension of benefits clause,* the insurance company the twins were covered under when they were born had to cover them for the duration of their hospital stay. The two insurance companies had been in communication. We will receive new statements reflecting our fully covered medical expenses in the next four to six weeks.

Compared to the ten million dollar bill we were almost on the hook for, whatever this rat smorgasbord is going to cost us doesn't seem so bad. We have two kids and no medical debt, so I will not waste my feelings on The Monster Truck. I never liked him anyway.

CHAPTER TWENTY-FIVE

Our Boy Who Lived

Some friends are for life, but most friends fare only for a season. When our grief takes up too much space or when we are drowning in murky waters of our own making, most people will back away—some much faster than others. If we're fortunate, we'll meet someone in the muck. Maybe they chose to dive in with us, or maybe life tossed them there. It doesn't really matter how they got there; when we encounter people who have been through the muck with us, we want to keep them forever.

June 21, 2021

    Off the northwest corner of our master bedroom is a rectangular space, hardly large enough to call a room. It has French doors and a window wall that lets in a light so dreamy I never questioned how strange it was to have a tiny room attached to the back of our bedroom. The tiny room was actually a selling point for me.
    I thought I would turn it into a reading room with a chaise lounge and a two-tier end table with a million tiny succulents on the bottom tier. I imagined a macramé

swing hanging in the corner and wall-mounted bookshelves. Then, I got pregnant. Glass, tangly tassels, and bookshelves that could double as a rock-climbing wall given a toddler's imagination seemed hazardous. And succulents, as low maintenance as they may be, were just another thing to keep alive.

The room sat vacant for a year after we bought the house, but for my 34th birthday I had one wish: to uncover who I was after all of this. I knew I didn't want my old self back. That girl didn't know anything about lung development or developmental milestones. She didn't know how to change a g-tube or cut a dragon fruit, let alone how to be a mother. I wouldn't go back for anything in the world. I am grateful to be a mother. Even so, I want more than motherhood. Being a good mother depends on me remembering I am something other than their *mamá*.

In the wake of a vaginal birth, a C-section, and a seven-month NICU stay, I had become someone I didn't know. My body was a different shape. I made friends with exhaustion, and my feelings—across the spectrum—were more intense than they had ever been. I needed to find my footing in this new self, and while I mean this metaphorically, I also mean it literally. I needed to move my feet, but I was too scared to run. I didn't want to be away from my daughters, and I wasn't in good enough shape to push extra pounds in a stroller. Instead of asking for my tried and true running shoes for my birthday, I asked Jerod for cycling shoes and a Peloton bike to go with them.

It's been 11 months since that Peloton was delivered and assembled in the tiny room. For the first five months it was here, I decorated the room around it. I put up wall decals and hanging plants—fake, of course. I assembled a storage unit, and rolled out a yoga mat neatly next to the bike, but I never used the actual bike. I was usually too tired, and if I did have the energy, I preferred to expend it on my daughters. There was also a discouragement factor. My pre-motherhood body was strong, flexible, and fast. This new body was none of those things, and I was preemptively disappointed in what it couldn't do.

In January, I made a commitment to start small. I rode for 10 minutes a day; it turned into 20. Now, I've been known to ride for an entire hour on the weekends, and I'm running again. It may be just a stationary bike, but the conquering of cardiovascular exercise reminded me that what I've been through may have rearranged my priorities and my organs, but it didn't break me.

My mom is here this afternoon, so I seize the opportunity and put on my workout clothes. I put on some socks and drop my phone into the cup holder of the bike. I am slipping my feet into the shoes that (against the manufacturer's advice) I've left clipped into the pedals when the phone rings. It's The Advocate. I silence the phone, thinking I'll call her back after my ride. On second thought, it's odd that she's calling. Between working crazy hours and raising babies, we usually have to plan our phone calls.

"Hello?" My greeting is a question.

"Hi, so," she holds the "o" and then pauses for way too long.

"There's a baby." She is probably going to explain something, but I interrupt her sentence with a gasp.

The Advocate was more than just my daughters' nurse. She was—and has continued to be—a good friend to me. When I was elbow-deep in diarrhea and frustrated with endless appointments, she had this way of validating what I was feeling while reminding me that almost everything is temporary and I am resilient. When I was tired, she brought green smoothies. When I was celebrating, she brought gifts. As our friendship evolved and I transitioned into a less tumultuous stage of life, she shared her tumult with me.

She and her husband spent years trying to conceive. This past spring, they started IVF, but when the initial evaluation came back, the doctor was pessimistic about the potential outcome. They decided not to move forward.

It didn't surprise me when The Advocate told me they were going to adopt. The way she has loved and championed my daughters as if they were her own babies is not something I'd ever seen anyone do. Most people are too busy trying to protect themselves to let themselves love this way. When she told me she and her husband were pursuing adoption, she asked me to write a letter of recommendation. I was honored, and I was emotional.

It takes a very open heart and a strong sense of responsibility to raise an adopted child with a solid sense of belonging, and I could not think of anyone more equipped than The Advocate. And now, it's happening!

"The thing is, he was just born—at 23 weeks," is all she says.

She expects my speechlessness, and she doesn't try fill the void. She knows I know exactly what this means. She knows, unlike her nurse and doctor friends—who see nothing but tubes, and trachs, and impending doom—I feel both heartache and hope.

"OK," I say. I feel faint; a chaise lounge would be ideal about now.

"Well, how do you feel about it?" It's the best question I can come up with, given the shock.

She is full of conflicting feelings and information. She knows the data and she's seen this end in tragedy, but she's also seen it end in Vivienne and Margot. She cannot help but believe that the way she loves my daughters is not a coincidence, but something of prophetic significance. She tells me there is a tiny boy, weighing exactly what my Vivienne weighed to the gram, in a hospital somewhere with no advocate. Everything in her is telling her she needs to be his support system.

Two years ago, her husband may have run in the other direction from the complexity of this case, but last year, he fell in love with my daughters. Now, he believes in impossible things. And she feels like it's her responsibility to ground him. If this story ends in death or a lifetime of grievous caretaking, she fears she will have robbed her husband of the fatherhood he imagined. The liability is crushing.

"No one—least of all me—will hold it against you if you don't choose this," I tell her.

She has been through so much already. She is already entering into a version of motherhood that was not what she planned. She has no obligation to make it even harder. With as many words as I usually have, they all seem insufficient now. I feel the weight of this decision. I am holding all the feelings about how this could play out—the beautiful expectations and the deep anguish—while trying to communicate that whatever decision she makes is the right one.

Despite the many questions I've had about God over the last couple of years, I still came out believing God is God, and we are not. Whatever control we think we have is an illusion. This would be enough to drive me mad if I didn't learn to trust that something omnipotent is holding the reins.

"It's an impossible decision," I tell her. "But know this: no matter what you choose you cannot mess it up."

When we get off the phone, I slip off my socks. I sit on the floor next to the bike. I cry and I laugh. I feel anxious and excited. I let myself experience this swirl of emotions. I smile as I remember myself as a numb new mother trying so hard not to love my daughters. I am not the woman I was.

The Advocate and I are in constant communication in the days that follow. She comes to an arrangement with the adoption agency and the social worker at the hospital to be there for this baby boy now, even though they are not ready to commit to adopting him. Her compassion is so unstinting that she cannot let this baby be alone, even if it means loving him only to lose him.

Without knowing whether this will be her son, she heads 200 miles south to be with him. She and her husband take turns sitting at this baby's bedside day and night, reading *Harry Potter and The Sorcerer's Stone* aloud. They name him Luca, a name they had reserved for their son. We are all praying he will be the boy who lives.

"Even if he's not our son," she tells me, "he will always be our Luca."

A month goes by, and Luca defies every odd. He should have brain damage from lack of oxygen because he wasn't born at the hospital and he wasn't intubated until he got there. But when the scan comes back, his brain is unharmed. Something should go wrong because, like The Possibility Doctor told me when my daughters were born, it is never an easy road for babies like them. They are holding their breath and I am holding mine as the milestones come and go and Luca conquers them one itty bitty gram at a time.

There are disagreements over Luca's course of treatment, the kind of disagreements that can only happen when your mother is a world-class micro preemie nurse. I want to believe my sorrow is as deep as his mother's when Luca fails his first extubation. And when the adoption paperwork is signed, we fight to get Luca transferred home. I use *we*, because I felt all of it. The intensity of my empathy does not exist to overpower The Advocate's emotions. It is, rather, a discovery about the depth of our friendship.

One hundred and forty days after Luca Anthony came into this world destined to be the love of Vivienne and Margot's lives, I sit in The Advocate's living room with her son in my arms. He is so tiny. It's hard to believe all three of our children were merely a sixth of this size when they were born. My daughters stare at him in awe, gently touching his head with their fingers. He is the very first baby they've ever seen. He is the very first baby they've ever loved.

As if to commemorate this happy day, Margot—who is a month away from her second birthday and has still not started walking—crawls over to a toy on the floor. She uses the toy as a crutch, and she stands up. We all grow quiet, but we realize how awkward we've made it for her, so we try to play it off by talking about her toy and not the fact that she's standing in the middle of the room. She smiles, and she takes three solid steps toward baby Luca. The crowd roars, minus the bundle of boy I'm holding who is a bit shaken by the excitement of it all.

This moment—two mothers, three children, none of them expected to survive; all of us thriving—is a picture of a new life. We were brought together in a long, dark winter, but in this living room we are ushering in a new season. Trials hurt us and change us, but what is shared between mothers in those desperate moments is the currency of lifelong friendship.

CHAPTER TWENTY-SIX

Guess Who's Back

Most sources say women's bodies usually recover from giving birth in six to eight weeks, which seems a bit rushed, but this is America—land of opportunity, not rest. Our hormones take longer to find equilibrium, and our hearts are never the same. Motherhood is wild and magical. It challenges our patience and our need for sleep and sustenance. Motherhood is lovely, but motherhood is brutal. It can make one feel quite unlike themselves.

September 2021

The Pregnant Dietitian is not pregnant anymore. She has a 15-month-old daughter, and she wants to train for a half marathon. She asks if I'd like to join her. I do, but I don't. It's complicated.

My kids don't sleep, so I practice intermittent exercise—hopping on the Peloton when the stars align and laying on the play mat resting my eyes when they don't. At the top of my priority list is keeping my children alive. Exercise falls somewhere after taking a shower and drinking enough water, neither of which happen regularly.

A perk of living the isolated life of a parent with immunocompromised kids is I don't feel pressure for my body to look a certain way. I look and feel different from the version of me that used to stand on my hands, but it takes most people 40 weeks to grow one baby and I grew two in 22 weeks. This new body is soft, but it's efficient. I am proud of it, and I need to take care of it.

When I tell The Not Pregnant Dietitian I'm in for the half marathon, it's not about the exercise as much as it is about taking a break from mothering to prioritize myself. Running carried me through the transition from college to the workforce. Running carried me through the loss of my first job and yoga saw me through the end of my first marriage. Everything that happens to us happens to our bodies. While it feels like the pre-motherhood version of myself has no place in this new life, she knew how to use her body to heal her mind. I'm taking that page from my history and making a commitment to physically put one foot in front of the other. It's a commitment to move through the trauma of my daughters' births and infancy and transition into the new person I've become.

I meet The Not Pregnant Dietitian and her two friends, The Baker and The Triathlete, at a park. We jog three leisurely miles around a lake in the heat of Florida's not-quite-fall, and it is relaxing. No one needs me. The rhythmic striking of my feet on the pavement is meditative. The parts of myself I thought I had lost when the vomiting and the fatigue of pregnancy took over have come back to life. I am Laura. Watch me run.

I am on an endorphin high when I get home. I want to clean the kitchen and head to the farmer's market. I want to bake bread and make vegetable broth from scratch. I make a meal plan and a grocery list. I devise a strategy so that we never have to order take out again. Maybe I've lost my mind, but maybe I'm back.

I am like a fashion influencer awaiting the Bloomingdale's Anniversary Sale during the seven sleeps between our Saturday morning training runs, but on Friday night, The Not Pregnant Dietitian sends a message in our group text that she can't make it. I had never met The Baker and The Triathlete before last week, and they've known each other a long time. A year and a half of prematurity-and-pandemic-induced isolation has made me socially awkward, and I wonder if I should skip this week. Part of me needs the familiarity of The Not Pregnant Dietitian as a social buffer, but the other part of me can't resist the opportunity to abandon my mothering responsibilities for an hour. I show up to run, and if I'm socially awkward, no one says anything about it.

The following weekend The Not Pregnant Dietitian can't make it and The Triathlete is on vacation. I run with The Baker, who is also a triathlete. I'm the only one of us who is not an Ironman, but that doesn't seem to matter. We are all older, slower, and softer than we used to be. Some of us have become mothers; some of us are trying to become mothers. We're all just putting one foot in front of the other in hopes of making it across the finish line and onto the next race.

On the fourth week, The Not Pregnant Dietitian sends a group text that reads, "So…" She waits an extra long time for dramatic effect before telling us she is The Pregnant Again Dietitian and will not be running the half marathon with us, but she promises she will be there to cheer us on. The timing of this announcement seems almost divine. Had she made this announcement during week two of our training, I probably would have stayed home. But now, I was registered for this race. Now, The Baker and The Triathlete were not strangers but running partners.

For 11 weeks, we show up and run. On the days when I think I cannot make it another mile, The Baker and The Triathlete tell me stories of their worst races. On the days they drag, I remind them they are freaking ironwomen, so they can most definitely make it one more mile. Most Saturdays, the miles are over before I'm ready to go back to my responsibilities. The weeks turn to months, and race day arrives almost suddenly.

It's five o'clock in the morning on December third. Jerod, always the supportive husband, drops us off at the start line. The streets of downtown Orlando are buzzing; this is the most people I've seen in one place since the pandemic started. I am nervous, or maybe excited. It's hard to tell. We line up. A brunette with a big voice belts the national anthem, and we're off.

The Triathlete and I stay together. Fueled by adrenaline, we finish the first three miles in 27 minutes. This is faster than we've finished any of our training miles. When the race map was published a few weeks ago, I saw the race wove through my neighborhood and right down my street. Just after the fourth mile marker, we turn into my neighborhood. I pick up my pace in anticipation. I pass a dozen of my fellow runners before I see my tiny toddlers armed with homemade pompoms. My mom, my aunt, and my husband stand at the end of our driveway with the girls cheering for *mamá*.

NOT WHAT I HAD IN MIND

Happy tears well as I approach. I have lived two unimaginable years. The lows were so low I didn't think I would live to see the highs. But this high is surreal. It was so unlikely Vivienne and Margot would stand together at the end of the driveway cheering for me that I couldn't have imagined it. The sight of them waving streamers between bouts of applause elicits a joy that reveals who I have become. I am a woman who strives to run 13.1 miles in under two hours. I'm also a woman who will gladly add 30 seconds to her race time to savor my daughters. I stop to hug them. "I'll see you at the finish line," I promise, and I keep running.

The high of my cheerleading squad carries me to mile six, where I realize I have to pee. I don't want to stop, though. My kids were worth the seconds I spent on them, but my urine? Not so much. By mile seven, The Triathlete runs ahead with a burst of energy; I fall behind with a burdensome bladder.

For 20 excruciating minutes I debate pissing myself. I worry about how my crotch will look in the finish line photos. Mustard yellow tights was a cute idea when I didn't have to pee in them. I don't think my bladder will carry me to the end of this race, but then I hear my name. I look up, and The Pregnant Again Dietitian is holding a huge sign over her belly. *Hey Laura, you spent 5376 hours in the NICU. You've got this two-hour run.* Yes! I have this two-hour run. I laugh, I cry, I pee a little, and at the next corner, I spot my mom cheering me on. My people at mile eight remind me of who I am. They carry me through to a portable toilet at mile 10. I've peed myself a bit and my legs are so heavy I can't even squat over the toilet. But somehow I finish the job, stand up, and press on.

I won't make my goal of running this race in under two hours, and I feel like a failure. If I had just stopped sooner to pee, I would have been so much more comfortable. I would have run all these miles so much faster. I get to mile 12 only by negotiating with myself: *If you run for three minutes, you can walk for 30 seconds.* It's not my body failing me, it's my head. When I realize I'm only a mile away, I dig deep for the will to keep running.

Somewhere in between miles 12 and 13, someone shouts my name. It's a woman I don't recognize. She's reading my name from my race bib, but when I look at her she says, "Oh my God, you're Laura with the twins." I nod, and I think, *Yes, I'm Laura with the twins, and if those twins made it, so can I.* I turn the corner to see the finish line in all its glory. I see my kids, my husband, and that most supportive mother of mine, and I pick up speed. I cross the finish line with enough vigor to jump for joy. My official time is two hours, five minutes, and 24 seconds, and I'm proud of myself.

I scoop Vivienne and Margot into my tired arms for a photo op. They are only interested in the rainbow medal around my neck. They don't know I've just reclaimed a piece of myself. They only know I'm their mother. We walk nearly half a mile down the street to the car against the flow of the race. I cheer on the runners who are still making their way to the finish line. I tell Jerod about The Pregnant Again Dietitian's sign and the woman who called me *Laura with the twins*. I climb into the backseat of the car effortlessly. This body is awesome.

If I have enough grit to train and enough endurance to finish this race, I can do anything. Seeing this race through to the end marks a transition into a new season.

NOT WHAT I HAD IN MIND

For two years, I have not been able to distinguish where my daughters end and I begin, but I see the edges of myself now.

The postpartum identity crisis is part of our evolution as mothers. We spend our whole lives trying to become a certain person. We have careers, routines, and hobbies. We have sleep habits and social lives, and then we don't. Motherhood is disruptive, and it can make us different and desperate for the women we once were. Our mom brains fear the sleep deprived, milk-making, bottle-washing, unclean version of ourselves is the only version left. We forget that everything has its season, but when the season starts to change, we realize we can be both mother and something other than.

CHAPTER TWENTY-SEVEN

Holy, Human, and Whole Grain

When we dedicate ourselves to something—or someone—we get sensitive about our sacrifices. The decision to rear children full time is more than a choice. It's the indefinite pausing of a career. It's the forfeiting of leisure time. It is the death of the person we used to be. As we try to uncover who this new mothering version of ourselves is, we may cling to the diapers we change, the books we read, and the meals we prepare. We may seethe or sulk at lighthearted comments about the literature we've selected or the lemon tahini pasta we've served, because when you're sacrificing yourself on the altar of family, it's all personal.

December 17, 2021

We are gathered around my parents' dining room table to celebrate Margot's second birthday. This lively little girl with big hair, bright brown eyes, and pink glasses is nothing like what the obstetrician told us she might be like. She walks, talks, and feeds herself. She pretends she is going to share her food with you; then she pulls it away from your mouth and eats it. She calls this a trick, and she finds it hilarious. We not only entertain this show, we think it makes her a genius.

My mom sets Margot's chair atop the formal dining table, and we gather round to sing. The Advocate, Luca, and our family came together to celebrate Vivienne's birthday two days ago, and they are all here again to celebrate Margot. Who doesn't love two children's birthday parties two days apart in the middle of the week?

I prefer birthday experiences to parties, so until my daughters can express their preferences, we will be adventurers. For Vivienne's birthday we went to the botanical gardens, complete with a splash pad and a vegetable garden. Today, we'll take a boat tour of the City of Winter Park, but first we will eat cake. Well, first we will eat salad, butternut squash soup, and beet hummus; then we will eat cake.

I've spent weeks researching dairy-free, egg-free, sugar-free cookies and cakes because birthday treats are tradition, and I don't want anyone thinking I'm depriving my daughters. Also, why else would a bunch of adults come to a two-year-old's birthday party if not for the cake?

While I am not one to cling to tradition, I confess, I want the pictures and the videos of my toddlers shoving fistfuls of homemade cake into their mouths. But, the Dietary Guidelines for Americans recommend no added sugar before the age of two. To err on the side of health, we will avoid sugar until the twins are at least 22. Thus, I am serving cake made from oatmeal, bananas, and flax meal. I frosted it with blended sweet potato, cashews, cacao, and dates. I also made plant-based oatmeal cookies, sweetened with bananas. They taste great, but it *is* a bit of a stretch to call them cookies.

Cooking and baking for my daughters has heightened my creativity. Finding recipes with foods we've never tried and making staples from scratch is time consuming, but its payoff has been incredible. My kids have better digestion and stronger immune systems than any of their specialists expected, and everyone agrees it's the food. But I'm learning these results are not as exciting for everyone else as they are for me. Not everyone is so quick to embrace cashews as cheese and butternut squash as edible.

Jerod is encouraging his mom to try the butternut squash soup, and she really doesn't want to. I know most people prefer the foods they grew up eating; this is not a culinary failure on my part, but it feels like one. I prepare food with the utmost attention to texture and flavor, not just for my daughters' health, but for my friends' and family's pleasure. I want my kids to share meals with their friends, and their grandparents, aunts, uncles, and cousins. I want to bring people together. I want us to share in the joy.

On the rare occasion that we have a playdate, I take food for the twins. I always bring extra to offer our friends; half the time they decline. I know how this looks because my friends always get a little twitchy. They ask if it's OK for their kids to eat cheese crackers. (Of course it is!) Sometimes, they explain their snack choice, as if to say *please don't judge my parenting based on this snack*. Food has the power to create wonderful shared experiences; it also has the power to make things awkward.

When the twins were 18 months old, my father-in-law promised them that when they came to visit him at his house, he'd make hot dogs. It was supposed to be funny but I felt like I had given up my life to spend my mornings steaming vegetables and my afternoons puréeing them. I had a spreadsheet (courtesy of my father) of the 83 vegetables we had on rotation to ensure the girls were getting enough plant diversity. It wasn't funny to me. It reinforced the narrative I had on repeat in my head: *I have to prove that what we eat is not strange, nor insufficient, nor unpleasant. I have to prove this is both scientific and delicious. I have to prove myself.*

Those who have watched our story unfold see my daughters walk and talk like normal two-year-olds, and they tell me what a miracle they are. My daughters elicit an unparalleled sense of wonder. I don't think it was a coincidence that no one brought me the DNR. I believe it was miraculous, but sometimes the talk of miracles is irritating. Sure, sometimes miracles are magical—like the DNR that never came—but most often, God does miracles through people who will fight for what they believe is right and what they believe is possible.

I've been fighting for my girls and for myself for two years. I sit them in front of a low-wavelength red light for therapy every night in hopes it will reduce the appearance of scars, improve their eye health, and help them sleep better. I have spent a thousand hours outside this year for fresh air and microbial diversity from the soil. I planted a garden. We mostly avoid pesticides, and I encourage them to chew kale leaves right from the plant. Of all the rituals I have adopted to set my daughters up for long, healthy lives, their diet is the most effective and the most challenging.

In the American grocery store, food is hardly food at all anymore. While the Dietary Guidelines for Americans say babies shouldn't have sugar, there is sugar in places it shouldn't be. I find it in hummus and in bread. I find it in oat milk and in cashew yogurt. Nothing is sacred.

I can't trust anything that comes prepared, so I buy dry beans. I soak them. I rinse them. I pressure cook them; I blend them with organic tahini and garlic to make hummus. I pack food every time I leave the house. These extremes are why Margot's short bowel symptoms are managed by diet alone. But the only person who is tracking the improvement of my kids' poop is me.

People look at our lives and see two perfectly healthy little girls whose mother is neurotic in her avoidance of sugar and partially hydrogenated oils. They don't change the diapers and they don't read the bloodwork results. They don't notice the way Vivienne and Margot ask for bowl after bowl of creamy spinach and tofu served over a bed of quinoa. What they see is plates of foods they have never heard of, and this freaks some people out. In their discomfort, they make jokes that I should be able to laugh off, but I can't because I am trying so hard to prove I am the right mom for the job.

I worry about what kind of relationship my daughters will have with food. The very society that celebrates peanut butter cup breakfast cereal will turn around and fat shame the women they believe ate too much of it. I am terrified my gospel of leafy greens and lentils will be distorted into some kind of diet culture dilemma. I fear the way tweens and teens moralize food around the lunch table. I worry my daughters will one day discover cheesy puffs or candy-coated chocolate pieces and gorge themselves, and I simultaneously worry they will be afraid to indulge. This is the tension of parenting: whatever good you do may also be bad, depending on how your children experience and understand the world.

Vivienne and Margot are here and they are healthy. It seems magical and miraculous that their brains and their bodies worked together to become typical toddlers. Some of their story is holy, but some of it is human.

My daughters are thriving because The Possibility Doctor, The Actual MD, and The Real Life Arizona Robbins went to school for a hundred and two years and studied under great doctors, and good doctors, and probably some truly mediocre doctors who shaped them into doctors who helped heal my kids. My daughters are here because, on the night of their bowel perforations, Perfect Eyeliner called the doctor and insisted they were not well. They are here because of the confident nurse who rang the code bell and gave chest compressions to bring Margot back to life. They are here because of the respiratory therapist who was on her way out the door—backpack on her back, water bottle in hand—when Vivienne's ventilator malfunctioned. She dropped everything to pump breath into my daughter's lungs. They are here because The Godfather made the right calls at the right times. My daughters are here by the grace of God, but it wasn't magic. The miracle was both supernatural and mortal. The miracle was a medical team that believed they could live. The miracle is I am their mother.

My life is lived in service to my children. I am consuming literature, collaborating with doctors, and cooking more than I'm sleeping. I am desperate to be seen as the mother I went through hell to become, instead of as that weird lady who only serves uncommon vegetables for dinner.

I know I can't control people. I know no one is trying to hurt me, but life, and motherhood, and therapy have made me soft. My identity, once rooted in my professional accomplishments and physical fitness, is now sitting at the bottom of a bowl of butternut squash soup. And I really need everyone to see what I had to overcome to make that bowl of soup happen.

We sing, "Happy Birthday, dear Margot. Happy Birthday to you." My mom helps Margot blow out her candles because if we wait for her to do it herself, the cake will be ruined and the house will turn to ashes. The crowd goes wild, and I wipe tears of joy from under my glasses with a pink cocktail napkin.

I can't imagine it will always be this way. The shock of our plant-based life will wear off. I'll stay in therapy until I find an identity grounded in something deeper than dinner. I am hopeful my sensitivity will level out, but until then, it would be great if everyone could just choke down the "cookies."

CHAPTER TWENTY-EIGHT

Baby's First Cold

We want to protect our children from everything that could hurt them, and what we see as a threat is determined by our subjective experience. Even the most laissez-faire parents work to protect their children from the types of people and situations that hurt them when they were children. If we suffered religious trauma, maybe we choose not to raise our kids in church. If we broke a wrist rollerblading, we are militant about safety gear. If we spent 224 days in a neonatal intensive care unit, the hospital is the danger we strive to avoid.

July 2022

Margot and I are in the waiting room of the Emergency Department at Orlando Health Arnold Palmer Hospital for Children. While my daughters were born across the street, *this* is the hospital that disassembled them and put them back together again. Down the hall, the phlebotomists have drawn their blood and collected their sweat in tiny vials to be tested. Upstairs is the operating room where, two months ago, the ophthalmologist and his team wheeled Margot back for eye surgery. She screamed for me all the way down the hall. I'm sure she didn't stop until she was sedated. I cried and shopped online for skincare and stuffed animals to cope while I waited to hear that surgery was a success.

It is one thing to send a blissfully unaware infant back to surgery; it is another to send a toddler screaming for her mother. We use the word gut-wrenching to mean something is upsetting. At the root of the word *wrenching* is the word *wrench:* a tool with jaws at one end and handles at the other to allow one to twist with great force. One might use a wrench to violently twist and remove a stubborn bolt. My daughter's screams left my insides violently twisted.

I love this place because my kids would not be alive without it, but—on days like today—it shakes loose all the anxiety I've worked so hard to control. The sterility and the sound of the Ease app ringing with updates make me want to vomit.

Margot woke up with her first runny nose this morning. By afternoon, she was coughing. This evening, I was watching her chest and her ribcage while she slept. I didn't like what I was seeing; that's why we ended up here. Seeing as how we still have next to no social life, it's safe to assume Margot's snotty nose and labored breathing are a byproduct of the dirty chairs she licked at the ophthalmologist's office on Tuesday. One day she will learn I was right about almost everything, but today, she does not regret licking those seats.

The coronavirus pandemic is still here, and I do not mess around with germs. We are ultra cautious, screening everyone for illness before we finalize plans. We meet friends and family outdoors, and we stay far away from the other patients in waiting rooms. I have two immunocompromised daughters.

Immune comes from Latin and means exempt from—as in, exempt from taxes or public service. In medicine, the word *immune* indicates exemption from a disease due to vaccination or because you contracted the disease and developed antibodies, thus reducing the likelihood of reinfection. In English, the word *compromised* has a few meanings, one of which means that something is weakened. To be immunocompromised means one's exemption from disease is weakened. In the case of my daughters, barring the diseases they've been vaccinated against, their exemption from disease is nonexistent.

A baby's immune system, which protects the body against microbial invasions, mostly develops in the third trimester. Antibodies from the mother cross the placenta and make their way to the baby. Vivienne and Margot never made it to the third trimester. They never got my antibodies. This is truly a shame because I rarely fall ill. However, just because they missed out on my super immunity, does not mean my daughters are destined for a life lived in a bubble. We want them to get sick. We want them to accrue antibodies, but the cost of those antibodies could be a stay in the pediatric intensive care unit.

In my thorough, albeit unprofessional, study of the gut microbiome, I learned microbial diversity is a pretty good indicator of overall health, including the health of one's immune system. There is a part of me that hopes I can feed my kids enough Swiss chard and sorghum to make up for the antibodies they did not get in utero. I imagine a world in which my kids eat so much spinach that viruses flee from them. While a healthy gut microbiome is a powerful tool for fighting illness, my dreams of preventing the common cold with leafy greens are unscientific.

From the outside, it looks like my daughters developed just fine in those slow cookers, but their insides look different from a typical toddler. Underdeveloped lungs kept open with high frequency ventilators are complicated. A ventilator keeps the lungs open, but it simultaneously damages them. The girls' airways and the tissue in the tiny air sacs that comprise the lungs took a beating; the result is bronchopulmonary dysplasia (BPD).

The symptoms of BPD can range from severe to almost nonexistent. The twins have not had trouble with their lungs since they were discharged—at least they hadn't, until they licked the waiting room chairs and caught themselves a respiratory virus. The quick and desperate breaths Margot is taking could be no big deal, or it could be the lasting effects of her prematurity.

For two and a half years, we've lived in fear of what can happen if our daughters get a cold before their lungs have grown big and strong enough to handle it. We've kept our family home. We've drawn hard boundaries about who can see our kids and where our friends and family can and cannot go if they want to spend time with the girls. We've drawn boundaries because we didn't want to end up here, being poked and swabbed in an emergency department full of sick kids.

A nurse takes Margot's temperature. The thermometer reads 104 degrees. I'm confused because my thermometer at home read just 101. I am ashamed I did not know how high her fever was. I want to cry, but I am the mother here. I need to keep it together.

The nurse administers ibuprofen and sweetly suggests I buy a better thermometer. Someone takes us back to a room where another nurse swabs Margot's nose for coronavirus, RSV, and flu. Before I came to the ED, I texted The Possibility Doctor and his wife, who is now one of my dearest friends. They told me to ask for a full viral panel. It won't change her course of treatment, but if we know what she has, we know how severe the virus is. It gives us an idea of what her lungs can handle and what they can't.

The nurse tells me it's not standard practice to get a full viral panel. She insists I don't need it. When the doctor comes in, I ask again. He asks me if I work in healthcare. I laugh and tell him I would if they gave out honorary medical degrees for living in a hospital for seven and a half months. He orders my full panel. He tells me he suspects Margot's labored breathing was because of her high fever. Her lungs sound great. I hold back tears of relief. He says he is still going to get an X-ray because, no matter how great she sounds, she is an ex-23-weeker.

The X-ray tech takes us back to a dark room with a futuristic bed. She tells me about how her daughter was also a preemie, 32 weeks. I try to smile in solidarity, but my heart is racing. I know Margot will be OK, but my body remembers when she wasn't. I put on the radiation armor provided for parents and I worry (yet again) about all the radiation my kids have gotten in their little lives. I vow to feed her all the antioxidants every day once we get out of here.

I hold Margot's hands over her head. Before she can process the situation and decide she hates it, we're done. We go back to our room in the emergency department where they give me a prescription for albuterol, an inhaled steroid, just in case she has any more trouble breathing. She probably won't, as everything has been normal since the ibuprofen kicked in. I can see the headline now: "Mom of the year takes her two-year-old to the ED for a dose of ibuprofen."

I am deep in my self-loathing spiral over how this could have been avoided if I had put the expensive thermometer on my baby registry. If I had the right thermometer and better judgment about when to give my kids a fever reducer, we'd be home sleeping right now. I have one arm wrapped around Margot in the hospital bed and I'm pressing my index and middle finger to my forehead in frustration when the doctor comes in to review Margot's viral panel results.

It's parainfluenza virus type three, a cousin to the dreaded RSV. Rest, fluids, ibuprofen, and acetaminophen are the recommended course of treatment. He reassures me that coming here was the right decision. "It is always better to be cautious," he tells me. Then, casually, as if it's not the most beautiful thing I've ever heard, he tells me my daughter's X-ray looked more or less like that of any sick kid. "You would never know she was born at 23 weeks." He says it matter-of-factly, like if it's to be expected. But it wasn't expected.

He doesn't know that Jerod watched Margot die and come back to life. He doesn't know I cried and prayed over her little body for days and nights on end as she withdrew from sedatives. He has never loved a baby who almost didn't live, so he talks about my daughter's (almost) typical lungs like they are no big deal.

I told my therapist this week that I live with the constant feeling that the other shoe is going to drop. Any time we so much as talk about trying something new, like swimming lessons, I think *this is it. This is going to be the thing they can't do because of their prematurity. This is going to be where I find out they are not like their peers. This is going to be what kills them.*

Every time I expose myself and my children to microbes from the outside world, I feel the tickle of viral doom in the back of my throat. *This is the germ that's going to kill them—or at the very least put us back in the hospital.* The Moms' Therapist asks me what will happen if they can't learn how to swim or if they need inhaled steroids for the rest of their lives. The whirl of invasive thoughts grinds to a halt.

It doesn't change anything if they can't swim or have to take medication. Nothing can devalue my daughters. Margot will still be funny, thoughtful, and brave. Vivienne will still be assertive, articulate, and quick. The real stressor is the assumption that the world will not understand. If they never learn to jump or read, or if they live with chronic illness, I worry the world will be unkind to them. This place is hazardous. Even the least anxious among us fears the wounds the world will inflict on the hearts of the people we made from scratch. We have all been hurt and we all anticipate the ways our babies will wind up wounded. We may have come to motherhood in different ways, but the hardest thing that's ever happened to you is the hardest thing that's ever happened to you, regardless of what happened to someone else. And those hardest things shape us.

Most parents probably don't fear death by common cold, and most parents probably don't live with the irrational fear their kids will never learn to swim, but we are all doing the same thing here. We are trying to protect our kids from getting hurt—physically, emotionally, spiritually—and we all have about the same amount of control, which is almost none. Our kids will grow up. We won't be with them every second of the day to tell them not to lick waiting room chairs or that tequila shots don't heal broken hearts. Motherhood is rooted in the need to raise humans who can navigate a wounded and wounding world and still appreciate its beauty.

CHAPTER TWENTY-NINE

Welcome to Motherhood

October 2022

Social media is a seductress, inviting us into comparison and dissatisfaction. For the last few years, I've taken long breaks from the influencer moms and the all-knowing advertisements because, while I love blowing money on silk pillowcases and lip stains, I know it's a distraction. However, nearly three years ago, I was desperate for distraction, specifically in the form of micro preemie twins who survived the NICU.

Social media is how I connected with Sarah. In the fall of 2019, Sarah brought home two tiny babies: James and Vivian. Sarah was on a trip to visit her family when her twins were born at 26 weeks gestation. They spent over 200 days combined in the NICU. Because Vivian needed a special MRI to diagnose a condition called colpocephaly, she was transferred to a different hospital, where she remained separated from her brother for the duration of her NICU stay. Like me, Sarah lived a traumatic birth followed by her heart and her body being pulled to different places. Sarah's suffering and her laments seem unfathomable to most, but to me they are #relatable.

Over the last two years, social media messages with Sarah turned into text messages, voice memos, and phone calls. We've swapped heartaches and recipes. We've become true friends, holding each others' anxieties and celebrating each others' victories.

This morning Sarah sends me a long message that turns into a voice memo that turns into a phone call. She asks me to connect with her friend Kim, who is in labor with identical twin girls—mono/di, just like Vivienne and Margot. Kim is 22 weeks and 1 day pregnant, and the hospital where she is admitted is painting the grim picture hospitals do when babies like ours cause trouble. They've told her 22-weekers don't survive.

When I pick up my phone to call Sarah, a memory popped up—a photo of The Godfather holding the twins on our first visit back to the hospital after discharge. I remember he shared that photo on social media after we took it. The caption read: *thank you Lord for allowing me to do your work. I love my job.* The contrast between this memory and what Kim is up against baffles me. How can physicians work with old research and no hope?

In talking to Sarah, the pit of my stomach feels like a black hole, sucking my guts and my soul and everything good out of my life. For a moment, I feel so ill it's like I am the one who was just told my daughters would be born 18 weeks too soon, like I am the one whose daughters have just been given a death sentence. I *feel* like I am the one whose daughters are unlikely to survive because I *was* the one whose daughters were unlikely to survive. Sarah's voice brings me back to reality. Her eagerness to help reminds me that our stories demand we step into these dire places to show moms like Kim they are not alone.

Sarah's panic is palpable as she explains the hospital refuses to give Kim steroids for the babies' lungs or magnesium to protect their brains.

"I know you don't want to stress her out," I message Sarah, imagining how I would have handled someone telling me I needed to fight for things I didn't understand, "but it's scientifically proven steroids and magnesium improve outcomes in micro preemies." I text my network of neonatal professionals to confirm this factoid before sending it.

Kim has no obligation to fight. I understand if she doesn't because I would not have been able to. Had I been at a different hospital, I don't know that I would have reached out to anyone. I wouldn't have known who to talk to. I wouldn't have known there were differing opinions on viability. If I had been at a hospital that had told me my daughters were going to die, they would have died. And if someone across the country who I had never met had told me I could fight for them, I don't know if I would have had the will. If Kim doesn't have the will, I will not impose on her. Self-preservation is sacred.

I tell Sarah I will talk to Kim. I will listen if that's what she needs, and I will fight alongside her if that's what she wants. We are united in our desire to fight for these babies and our commitment to support Kim no matter what she chooses. But Sarah seems sure Kim is ready to fight.

When I talk to Kim, she has already decided to resuscitate her daughters. She does not stop asking for steroids and magnesium until someone with enough power agrees to administer them. I am in awe of the way she has advocated for herself and her daughters. For days, we exchange communication in all forms. I feel her fears and her premature grief in a way only a mother of periviable children can. I want to offer her hope, but I'm afraid for her to hope too much. I'm afraid hope is too high a hill to fall from when things fall apart. All I can offer her is the promise that this will be unbearable. It will be the hardest thing she has ever done, and it will reveal to her what she is made of.

"I feel like I'm going to have guilt either way. It's like no matter what, I am going to make the wrong choice," Kim tells me.

She's right. She will feel guilty when she sees her tiny daughters hooked up to machines or screaming their heads off during physical therapy. Whether she has to see the scars of prematurity on her daughters' bodies or she never gets to, she may feel guilty for the rest of her life. But I know that guilt will evolve. If they live, she will know they are here because she fought for them; if they don't, she will know she gave them a chance. My prayer is that her guilt and her weeping will turn into songs of joy one day.

Friday blurs into Monday, and in the early hours of the morning Kim goes into labor and quickly delivers two baby girls. I'm in the middle of making dinner when I get the news: Amelia was born sleeping. I drop my wood spoon covered in creamy grits on the counter and I walk through the living room where my aunt is playing with my girls. I make my way into my bedroom. I close the door and lay prone on the floor, the way I did the day Vivienne and Margot's bowels perforated. I scream into the floor, which I know from experience is the only place to look for God in times of suffering. *Please let Quinn live.*

In the following days, Kim's messages to me are sporadic. I can feel her frustration when she explains that every neonatologist and nurse she's talked to has told her, "most babies like Quinn don't survive." She is mere days postpartum when she fires back.

"Most babies means the majority—and the majority of babies born at 22 weeks at the University of Iowa do survive. So if your survival rates are low, you better get help from a hospital with better outcomes," she tells them.

Kim is a wonder. This mother who just lost a baby and has another barely clinging to life is telling Ivy League doctors where to shove it, respectfully.

Fall becomes winter, which in Florida means nothing, but in Connecticut marks a change in seasons, and Quinn changes, too. She is a blonde beauty, so perfect that she reminds me of Vivienne and Margot's prettiest baby dolls. Every time the doctors tell Kim and her husband to say their goodbyes, Quinn laughs and takes an alternate route. There is no doubt she has declared herself. She has grown into a three-pound baby. But her lungs are not growing with her.

"These are not choices I should have to make," Kim says to me.

Quinn is 109 days old and Kim is researching if she should (and how she would) get her transferred to a hospital that specializes in severe bronchopulmonary dysplasia. The hospital where she and Amelia were born intervenes at 22 weeks gestation at the parents' insistence, but they've reached the limits of their knowledge and resources. Here is this mother who has not had space or time to grieve the loss of her firstborn daughter, contemplating a move halfway across the country to give her second-born daughter a better chance at life. I'm embarrassed by how severely I underestimated Kim's will and capacity to fight.

This isn't the way it's supposed to be. These aren't decisions parents should have to make. She is traversing the Wild West of motherhood, and the wildest thing about it is she would do it all again.

"All children are worth fighting for," she tells me.

She explains she would never judge anyone for making a different choice than she did. Everyone has a different capacity. She says the prematurity and this extended NICU stay has revealed she is much more capable than she thought she was. She is *way* more capable than I thought she was, and it makes me wonder if I underestimate myself. I've been believing that, in an alternate version of my story, I would have just held Vivienne and Margot while they died. But maybe that's not true. Maybe I would have fought like Kayla or learned quickly so I could advocate like Kim. Maybe I would have gotten second and third opinions like Sarah did when a doctor recommended a surgery she wasn't convinced her Vivian needed.

I know a mother who has traveled the world seeking alternative treatments for her son who suffered a severe brain injury after he and his twin sister were in a near-fatal drowning. My friend Ryen's three-year-old daughter was diagnosed with Leukemia. While she started out trying to keep the peace, she reached her limit when a new nurse was stabbing and *digging* around for a port that was just under the skin. Sweet, non-confrontational Ryen yelled at the nurse to stop. Not only did she do the legwork to find a nurse who knew how to access a port, but she demanded better care for all patients with ports. We may start this experience of motherhood with differing comfort with confrontation, but when we need to, we all land in the arena ready to fight.

Kim wishes she had been more informed going into this horror. She wishes she had known about periviability and which hospitals in her area had the best outcomes for extremely premature babies. Maybe she would have gone somewhere else. Maybe she would have moved to Iowa. Trauma messes with your brain and it's hard to make these life-altering calls about your children when you have to process new, complicated information to make the decisions. Hearing her say this hits me hard.

We live in a time of information overload, but in trying times, we can rarely find the information we need—and if we do, we still have to distinguish truth from misinformation. Whether we're researching periviablity or learning disabilities, what we find leaves our hearts pounding and our heads spinning.

In the aftermath of our NICU stay, I pushed myself into the lives of our medical team. I sent birthday gifts and baby gifts. I sent milestone updates and New Year's cards. Our team of physicians, nurses, and respiratory therapists became my family, and as over the top as my gratitude for them may have seemed at first, it cultivated meaningful relationships. One of the most profound relationships that came from our NICU time is my relationship with The Possibility Doctor's Wife. She has become My Confidant.

When I found out The Possibility Doctor and his wife were expecting a baby girl, I was overjoyed. I delivered boxes full of my very favorite clothes the twins had outgrown. And when their daughter was born, I delivered a gift bag full of disposable underwear, herb-infused maxi pads, and a pumping bra—a tradition inspired by The Often Pregnant Dietitian. It was a risk to send a stranger feminine hygiene products, but the payoff had great potential.

We are raising our three daughters together. We've swapped meals, and cooties, and bathed each other's babies. When I am at my worst—when I scream at my daughters or cry into the floor—it's My Confidant who receives my confessions with empathy.

When Kim first reached out to me about Amelia and Quinn, I called My Confidant. She is a pediatric and neonatal dietitian who used to work at the hospital where Kim's daughters were born. She had no stakes in this woman's story, but she helped me gather insider information to help Kim advocate for herself.

When My Confidant was 16 weeks pregnant with her daughter, she called her OB's office to request an ultrasound because she was, "very anxious." The nurse who returned her call said to her, "Welcome to motherhood. You're going to feel this way the rest of your life." Ain't that the truth?

The burden Kim is carrying as she navigates how best to advocate for Quinn is unfair when juxtaposed with a textbook pregnancy and delivery. I know the loneliness and resentment that come from months steeped in trauma. I know the compulsion to stifle hope in anticipation that it will all fall apart. It feels inevitable that wet tissue paper will tear. But I also know a mother's condition is dynamic. I know that even in the midst and in the aftermath of impossible circumstances, we will find people who will share in the constant anxiety of motherhood with us.

Quinn got her transfer to the hospital with a dedicated BPD unit, and it may save her life. It will be a long road for our warrior and her mother, and there are no guarantees, but there would be no road without a mother like Kim.

The most interesting part of motherhood is the empathy it fosters. The moment we become mothers, we gain an ability to feel the depths of another mother's anxiety or grief in a way no other group of people share. When we are stuck in the seam of desperation, it obstructs our view of how deeply fellow mothers feel for us. But even the foggiest places on earth have a clear day occasionally. It's on those days we can allow ourselves a moment of lightness, knowing we are not in this alone.

CHAPTER THIRTY

All of the Scars

The full responsibility of parenting is unfathomable to the new or expectant parent. It is probably not until we watch our children function as adults in the big, scary world without us that we can see how we shaped them. But the weight of this responsibility gets heavier the more we watch our children watch us.

January 2023

    The musical stylings of last year's hottest animated film blare through my car's stereo to keep the three-year-olds awake. It's 4 p.m. on a Tuesday afternoon, and if they fall asleep right now, there will be no peace on earth—no goodwill for them.

    As I pull into the driveway, Vivienne is snoring in her car seat. *Why, God? Why?* I don't have the heart to wake her up, so I unleash Margot. I stand outside of my still-running vehicle and perform a quick internet search. *Can I leave my kid in my running car in my driveway for just a second?* The answer is a hard no. *Cool.*

Dinner time is rapidly approaching, and all I have to do is transfer the meal I prepared this morning from the refrigerator to the stove. If I can let this kid sleep for 10 minutes while I do that, my life will be a little easier. I leave the car running with all the windows open; I leave the front door of the house open, giving me a clear view of the car. *Technically, I am supervising her, so this is not illegal, right? How do other moms handle this?*

I grab my Dutch oven, spices, a resealable bag full of pre-cut vegetables, and a bottle of avocado oil and I stand in the front doorway preparing dinner with my eyes on the vehicle where Vivienne sleeps. Once everything is in the pot, I make a mad dash back to the stove, light it, I turn the knob to the lowest setting, and head to the car to wake Vivienne up.

With Margot pulling at my pant leg screaming, "Wake up, Vivi," I unbuckle my sleepy little girl and carry her to the kitchen; her sister follows behind us. When I step into the house, I take a deep inhale, appreciating that just-cleaned smell our trusted cleaning lady leaves in her wake, and I panic. Along with the fresh scent of lemon oil, I smell gas. I put Vivienne on the ground and tell her and her sister to wait by the dining room table and not to move. They can sense my panic because they whimper as I dart away.

When I walk into the kitchen, I see the stove is not lit and the burner cap is not sitting flush with the burner. It's a simple mistake to make when you've disassembled a stove to clean. But now, to turn off the gas, I have to pass through the lighter setting. It's inevitable, I am going to cause a fire for a second—at least I hope it's only for a second. *I should have noticed the stove didn't light when I turned it on. I shouldn't have tried to get dinner ready while my kid was sleeping in the driveway. I should have done this differently.*

I quickly sit Vivienne and Margot on the far side of the room in chairs and tell them not to move. I turn the knob to shut off the burner and immediately pull my hand back. As expected, the stove lights up in a show of flames that disappears as quickly as it arose. The hair on my arms is mildly singed, but we survived the great gas fire of 2023. I open the doors and windows to air out the house. I check all the burner caps and start dinner for real.

As the vegetables simmer, I open the bottom of our two-tier pantry and search for the red lentils. I know Jerod bought them, but they aren't where I expect them to be. I open the top tier. It's just high enough that I have to stand on my toes to pull the bags of grains and legumes down to see what they are, and when I do, the clink of glass alerts me to the impending crisis. The bottle of ghost pepper sauce falls five and a half feet, shattering and splattering. *This cannot be my life right now.*

"Fucking. Fuck. Fuck," I say, immediately regretting my word choice in a room full of toddlers.

The analogy that kids' brains are like sponges may be overused, but it's accurate. I love the toddler stage. My daughters mimic behavior and language to make sense of the world. It is a marvel to experience their expanding vocabularies and the development of emotional intelligence. In their infancy, our relationship was one-sided, with them depending on me for everything, but now, they engage. I tell them stories and they want to tell me their stories. They narrate the world around them.

Our eyes are watering and we're coughing from the particles of ghost pepper sauce floating in the kitchen.

"Fuck," Vivienne says. I know better than to respond, so I ignore it, but she insists. "The glass fell, and *mamá* said fuck," she expounds on her statement. I bite my lip and turn my face away from her to stifle my laughter. I may not know much about parenting, but I know better than to give this any attention.

My daughter's first use of an expletive is hilarious and a little humiliating. A cursing toddler is funny, until it's not. If I needed a sign that it's time to control my tongue, this is it. But it's more than just what comes out of my mouth I have to think about.

We want to believe our kids are too little to notice the expletives we drop and the way we pinch our tummies or cover blemishes in the mirror, but my daughters are already asking me if I'm going to put on a lot of make up in the morning. They ask me to put creams on their faces and balm on their lips like *mamá*. What I choose to do to my face and my body will influence what my daughters believe is expected of their faces and their bodies.

Where most babies' bodies are smooth canvases, my daughters' bodies are forever etched by the wounds that made them warriors. Across their bellies, down their arms, and into the places most people will never see are reminders of how they fought to stay alive. It's a powerful story, but I fear it won't be powerful enough to combat societal beauty standards.

I am overdue for an appointment with my plastic surgery PA to inject a neuromodulator into my forehead to cause paralysis in the name of wrinkle prevention. I haven't made the appointment because I've been thinking about whether this is what I want to model for my children. This is not a question of morality. It may be futile to spend thousands of dollars trying to delay aging, seeing as how we're all going to die eventually, but it's not immoral. However, the message it sends is that we can change the parts of our bodies with which we are dissatisfied, and this may not be true for my daughters.

The surgery scars across their bellies and the deep grooves left by Vivienne's aspergillus infection may fade, but they won't go away. Society wants to believe its come a long way with diversity and average-sized models in clothing commercials, but I have yet to see an ex-lap scar on a bikini model. And it wrecks me to think my daughters could grow up believing they are anything less than beautiful because of the scars they will forever wear across their bodies.

Some parenting philosophies are so black and white: honor your mother, don't kill, don't steal, don't eat your sister's slice of sourdough bread. Other philosophies are a medium shade of gray: do we work with society's beauty standards to the best of our abilities, or do we exhaust ourselves trying to shatter them?

I would love to ignore the beauty myth the media perpetuates like I ignored Vivienne's profanity, but if I don't evaluate my profanity—or my idea of beauty—I worry my kids will get the wrong idea. I can't shield them from pop culture's body type *du jour*, but I can show them what it looks like to love themselves. My scars brought them into this world; their scars kept them alive. We ought not airbrush our way out of this.It's what makes the story a story.

In the words of Brandi Carlisle, "all of these lines across my face tell you the story of who I am." The way our stories mar us is nothing to be ashamed of. Scars announce to the world that we have truly lived. Does this mean I'm not scheduling an appointment with the PA? I don't know yet. I don't know how to navigate my pursuit of self-confidence in a way that minimizes damage to my daughters. (Let's face it, *minimize* is the best we can do.) No one comes out of childhood unscathed. To be fair, no one comes out of motherhood unscathed either.

Motherhood forced me to face what really matters, which turned out to be much less than I originally thought. I thought I would die atop the hills of Spanish language immersion and a sugar-free diet. I also thought I would birth two healthy little girls from my vagina. These are lovely hopes, but if I don't give my daughters everything I thought I would, if they grow up to speak improper Spanish and only eat pizza rolls, they will still be my most beloved. If they know this—if in their most despairing moments they can come back to the truth that they are always beautiful and unconditionally loved—I did my job. At least this is what I tell myself when I'm concealing my under-eye circles in the morning.

If we are lucky, we will parent our children for decades. In our children we will see our greatest victories and the errors of our ways. Our children will delight us and destroy us. They will torment us and teach us; they will stretch us to our limits and repeat our obscenities back to us. Just as much as we are shaping them, they are chipping away at our hearts, turning us into who we were meant to be. No matter how prepared we think we are, and no matter our origin story, motherhood is never what we had in mind.

ACKNOWLEDGEMENTS

This is a story I didn't think I would ever find the words or the format for. I spent a long time telling myself the world did not need another book about prematurity—and certainly not one by someone with no credentials. In many initial drafts, I tried to write myself out of the narrative. I know now that was an impulse born out of of fear and insecurity. To write this story, I had to lean into my darkest moments, and it was terrifying to think about what could happen if I published those moments for all to see. Possibly more terrifying was doing this work only for it to have no impact. Sometimes, these thoughts kept me from writing anything worthwhile; often they kept me from writing anything at all.

A phone call to my friend and fellow author, Asha Junot, in the summer of 2022 was the catalyst for this book. When I told her I was stuck and I was scared, she validated my fears and she told me to start writing and to stop thinking about what other people were going to do with it. She encouraged me to trust God to turn this book into what it needed to be. For that, I am forever grateful.

Without my editor, Katie Schmidt, this book would not exist. Her encouragement in the margins of the earliest manuscript was the fuel that kept me writing. She knows what I am capable of, and she held me to that standard throughout the creative process. I am a better writer and storyteller because of her brilliance. It is a pleasure to kill my darlings with her.

A huge thank you to my daughters' abuelo and abuela (Hi Dad! Hi Mom!) for always encouraging me to explore my stream of creative ideas. I am resilient, resourceful, passionate, and relentless because you raised me, and I could only write this book because you're helping raise my daughters.

Tia Lidia, every moment you spent with Vivi and Gogo so I could bring this book to life mattered to me and to them.

Thank you to Nicole Damico, Nicole Queliz, Brianna Burrus, Susie Bolton, and (again) Asha Junot for praying me through the shittiest first draft, and for your enthusiasm about this book's potential.

A very special thank you to LJ Hackler for sharing your unparalleled talent with me for the cover design of this book. There was never anyone else in mind for the job. Not only did you nail it, but you offered generous encouragement in my moments of insecurity.

I am full of gratitude for Kayla Ibarra and every voice in the prematurity community that has fought for babies like mine and reminded me that every story matters.

And to all our friends and family, I am forever thankful for your consistency. Your prayers, support, and the strength you lent us on our scariest, most desperate days were a reminder that—even if it felt lonely at times—we were never on our own.

To every nurse, respiratory therapist, and physician who put their hands on (or in) my daughters—or even thought about them—words will always fall short to express what you mean to me. Thank you for taking a chance on my girls. Thank you for being an integral part of this happy story.

To my husband Jerod, thank you for believing this story was worth the time and money we put into making it a reality. The many mornings you were late to work and the hundreds of nights you put our screaming children to bed were instrumental. Every time I thought I should give up because I couldn't find the time, energy, or will to navigate the process and logistics of this massive project, you showed up ready to do whatever it took to move it forward.

To my daughters. Your will to live is why there was a story to tell; you have given me perspective on what really matters.

Finally, from the story itself to the book that resulted, I have witnessed divine intervention after divine intervention. I am grateful to God for the mysterious—though, often brutal—ways he orchestrated this.

REFERENCES

Brown, Brené. Daring Greatly: How the Courage to Be Vulnerable Transforms the Way We Live, Love, Parent, and Lead. Gotham Books, 2012, pp. 1-2.

Bulsiewicz, Will. Fiber Fueled: The Plant-Based Gut Health Program for Losing Weight, Restoring Your Health, and Optimizing Your Microbiome. Avery, 2020.

Cook Children's Health Care System. "Cook Children's Preemies Program." Cook Children's Health Care System, 2021, https://www.cookchildrens.org/services/neonatology/specialty-programs/preemies/.

"EMDR Therapy: What Is EMDR?" EMDR International Association. Accessed April 11, 2023. https://www.emdr.com/what-is-emdr/.

"Esotropia." American Association for Pediatric Ophthalmology and Strabismus (AAPOS) - Glossary of Terms. Accessed April 11, 2023. https://aapos.org/glossary/esotropia.

Etymonline. (n.d.). In Online Etymology Dictionary. Retrieved April 11, 2023, from https://www.etymonline.com/

Hintz, Susan R., et al. "Impact of Gestational Age on Outcomes of <1000 g Birth Weight Infants with

Critical Congenital Heart Disease." The Journal of Pediatrics, vol. 209, 2019, pp. 128-134.e3, https://www.jpeds.com/article/S0022-3476(19)31216-8/fulltext.

The Holy Bible, New International Version. 1 Kings 3:16-28.

Johns Hopkins Medicine. "Intraventricular Hemorrhage (IVH)." Johns Hopkins Medicine, Johns Hopkins Medicine, 2021, https://www.hopkinsmedicine.org/health/conditions-and-diseases/intraventricular-hemorrhage.

Lurie, Susan. "Caesarean section in Ancient Greek mythology." Acta Med Hist Adriat, vol. 13, no. 1, 2015, pp. 209-16. PMID: 26203550.

Merriam-Webster. "Viable." Merriam-Webster, Merriam-Webster Inc., 2021, https://www.merriam-webster.com/dictionary/viable.

National Center for Biotechnology Information. Stoll, Barbara J., and Tricia Lacy Gomella. "Gestational Age and Birth Weight." Neonatology: Management, Procedures, On-Call Problems, Diseases, and Drugs, edited by Tricia Lacy Gomella et al., 8th ed., McGraw-Hill Education, 2016, https://www.ncbi.nlm.nih.gov/books/NBK234146/.

National Library of Medicine. "A Brief History of the Cesarean Section." NLM, National Institutes of Health, 2019, https://www.nlm.nih.gov/exhibition/cesarean/part1.html.

Online Etymology Dictionary. "Perinatal." Online Etymology Dictionary, Douglas Harper, 2021, https://www.etymonline.com/word/perinatal#etymonline_v_35890.

Pineda R, Bender J, Hall B, Shabosky L, Annecca A, Smith J. "Parent participation in the neonatal intensive care unit: Predictors and relationships to neurobehavior and developmental outcomes." Early Hum Dev, vol. 117, Feb. 2018, pp. 32-38. doi: 10.1016/j.

www.ingramcontent.com/pod-product-compliance
Lightning Source LLC
Chambersburg PA
CBHW050325010526
44119CB00038B/470/J